REALLY GREAT MOVIES FOR KIDS AND FAMILIES

common sense media's

BEST RATED DVDs

REALLY GREAT MOVIES FOR KIDS AND FAMILIES

---

common sense media's BEST RATED DVDs

By the Editors of
Common Sense Media

This guide was funded through the generous support of First Republic Bank, a proud sponsor of Common Sense Media

Common Sense Media
1550 Bryant Street, Suite 555
San Francisco, California 94103

www.commonsensemedia.org
Common Sense Media is a non-partisan, not for profit organization.
For further information, email us at info@commonsensemedia.org

First Edition
Printed in the United States of America
ISBN: 978-1-4276-2396-6

About This Guide

We know parents are the busiest people on earth. Sometimes there just isn't time to wade through thousands of movie choices, wondering which are best for family viewing. That's why this invaluable resource contains a highly selective list of titles. It's designed to be a big, rich recommended list rather than an exhaustive guide.

After reviewing thousands of movies, our editors have selected 150 DVDs with high entertainment value that are appropriate for kids ages three through fifteen (through middle school). And while there were literally hundreds more we loved, we can pretty much guarantee that the movies in these lists will please both kids and parents at every age and stage of development.

In this volume you'll find an alphabetical listing for each movie, movies arranged by recommended ages, and movies by genre and activity. The lists are designed with reality in mind: we offer just a few choices in each category because parents have told us they only want a couple of really great options when it comes to renting that perfect DVD. We also include thematic recommendations based on what our members at Common Sense have requested, like (Not Too) Scary Movies, Sleepover Movies, Father-Son Movies, Meaning-of-Life Lessons, and more.

We look forward to updating this guide annually, so we want to hear what you recommend. Just send us an email at info@commonsensemedia.org. Meanwhile, get the popcorn, sit back, and ENJOY!

About Our Ratings

Four- or five-star movies rated ON for a certain age? What does that mean? It means a movie is of excellent quality *and* it's appropriate for the age we indicate. Unlike all the other major ratings systems in this country, the Common Sense Media ratings are grounded in child development principles established by some of the nation's leading experts.

When we look at a movie, we don't give it a simple thumbs up or down. Instead, we take the content of a movie and match it to different developmental stages for children. (We do this for every kind of media, by the way, not just movies; but you will find those reviews on our website.) Each movie rating has a minimum recommended age for which the movie is appropriate and whether or not it is an On (good for the age).

Our goal is to give you enough reliable information to determine what works for you. We know that all kids and families are different. Some thirteen-year-olds can handle complex emotional movies, others can't. Some six-year-olds readily grasp that a cartoon isn't reality when others take what they see as real. All families need transparent guidelines about age appropriate content so they can make up their minds for themselves. In all cases, there's no substitute for knowing your kids—each one is different, and all families have their own preferences.

This pocket guide makes it easy—it contains only those rated ON for certain ages. Some of the movies are simple, some a bit edgier. But all have full disclosure about what parents need to know before popping in a DVD and settling in to watch. Here are some tips:

- **Always do your homework.** Check ratings and content information before your kids see a movie. This is especially true if you are not going to watch with them. Many DVDs have 'extras' that aren't rated. There can be some unpleasant surprises in this material. Also, double-check ratings on DVDs because sometimes they are different than the theatrical releases due to added material.

- **Watch these movies with your kids.** There's nothing like having a special evening with the phone turned off and the popcorn ready to go. We have super wholesome movies for little kids that won't bore parents and more complex movies for those increasingly rare nights when your teens settle in to hang out with their folks. (We've included some edgier selections for older kids because watching a movie together can tee up a conversation about life you might not have otherwise.)
- **No movies for kids under two.** Don't buy into the "genius" stuff. There's not a shred of evidence anything on a screen helps infants and toddlers become smarter. In fact, all research points to the importance of human interaction at these tender developmental ages.
- **Determine what matters to you.** Not all content concerns are the same. But share your values with your kids. Tell them why you do or don't agree with certain kinds of movies. We all have different hot buttons and our kids need to know our individual value and moral systems.
- **Tell friends about your family's viewing rules.** Every family has different approaches. If you don't let your kids watch certain movies at home, make sure you share your sensitivities with the parents of your kids' friends.
- **These are great movies but don't sit around all day and watch them.**

About Common Sense Media

Every year, millions of parents turn to Common Sense Media for help in managing their families' media lives. It's a simple fact: In a world where kids now spend three hours watching TV and movies, texting, instant messaging, listening to music, and playing video games for every one hour they spend hanging out with their moms or dads. Media has become the other parent. At Common Sense Media, our mission is to help parents remain the primary influence in their kids' lives.

How do we do this? We give parents tools and information. We know parents can't be everywhere or know everything. They can't play every videogame, screen every movie, go on to every Web site. Instead, we give parents thousands of up-to-the minute reviews written expressly for them so that they have the information they need to decide what's right for their families. And while they're at it, parents get tips and tools to make sure kids aren't spending their whole lives sedentary and plugged in.

We believe parents are the experts—they just need quality trustworthy information to make the right decisions for their individual kids. And some of the biggest names in entertainment—Comcast, Time Warner Cable, Cox Communications, Best Buy, Disney, Netflix, AOL, MSN, TiVo (to name a few)—agree with us. They carry our reviews, ratings, tips, and recommendations to their customers because they trust our independent, child-centered point of view. Since we are a non-profit, non-partisan organization, people understand that our only purpose is to help families make the most of the powerful media that surrounds and informs our world.

Check us out at www.commonsensemedia.org. Join our community of caring parents who use their common sense when it comes to media and their kids.

Contents

THE BEST MOVIES: A TO Z **8**

MOVIES BY TOPIC **93**

Adventures **93** • Bad Boy Movies **93** • Baseball Movies **94** • Biopics **94** • Car Movies **95** • Classic Comedies **95** • Classic Sports Movies **96** • Classics Worth Making Your Kids Watch **96** • Coming-of-Age **97** • Dance Movies **97** • Documentaries **98** • Dog Movies **98** • Fairy-Tale Movies **99** • Family Musicals **99** • Fantasy Worlds **100** • Father-Son Stories **101** • First Movies **101** • Foreign Films **102** • Great African American Movies **103** • Great Classic, Great Remake **103** • Great Latino Movies **104** • Holiday Movies **104** • Literary Classics (Book-to-Screen) **105** • Magical Movies **107** • Meaning-of-Life Lessons **108** • Mother-Daughter Stories **108** • (Not Too) Scary Movies **109** • Offbeat Gems **109** • Pirate Movies **110** • Rock and Roll Movies **111** • Sleep-over Movies **111** • Space Movies **112** • Sports Movies **113** • Staring Live Animals **113** • Strong Girls **114** • Superhero Movies **115** • Talking about Loss **115** • Triumph of the Underdogs **116**

MOVIES BY GENRE **117**

Action/Adventure **117** • Animated **118** • Classics **121** • Comedy **122** • Documentary **125** • Drama **125** • Fantasy **128** • Musical **129** • Science Fiction **130**

MOVIES BY AGE AND STAGE **131**

Preschool and Kindergarten (2-5) **131** • Elementary School Years (6-10) **135** • Tweens, Teens, and Middle Schoolers (11-15) **140**

THE BEST MOVIES: A TO Z

101 Dalmatians

Lovable cartoon classic for all ages.

on 5+
★★★★★

Director: Clyde Geronimi, Hamilton Luske, Wolfgang Reitherman
Cast: Rod Taylor, Betty Lou Gerson, Cate Bauer **Running time:** 79 minutes
Theatrical release date: 1/25/1961 **Genre:** Animated **MPAA rating:** G

Parents will be lucky to escape their kids begging for a puppy after they fall in love with this animated Disney classic. The dog tale is told from the perspective of Dalmatians Pongo and Perdita and their pups as they struggle to stay together. Keep in mind that the young and impressionable may be unnerved by one of the most memorable villains in movie history, Cruella de Vil–who kidnaps the puppies to make herself a fur coat. Glenn Close played creepy Cruella in the 1997 live-action version, but the real dogs lack the expression of their animated predecessors. The characters are adorable, the movie is funny, and the story has managed to remain a favorite among young audiences over the years.

2001: A Space Odyssey

Kubrick's sci-fi masterpiece is still relevant.

on 12+
★★★★★

Director: Stanley Kubrick **Cast:** Keir Dullea, Gary Lockwood, William Sylvester **Running time:** 141 minutes **Theatrical release date:** 4/6/1968 **Genre:** Science Fiction **MPAA rating:** G

Here's a great introduction to sci-fi for thoughtful tweens and teens. This Kubrick classic (the most accessible one for kids) tracks mankind's journey from the dawn of man four million years ago to the exploration of deep space. You might want to warn them that this isn't a fast-paced spaceship movie with the latest special effects; it's more about pondering and appreciating the mysteries of life and the universe. Characters are in peril (some are killed), and there are some frightening messages about technology getting out of control (in other words, this is the thinking person's *Terminator*). There's a lot to talk about here, from the increasingly important role technology plays in our world to the movie's cryptic, much-discussed ending.

The Absent-Minded Professor

Family entertainment at its best.

on 6+

★★★★★

Director: Robert Stevenson **Cast:** Fred MacMurray, Nancy Olson, Keenan Wynn **Running time:** 97 minutes **Theatrical release date:** 3/16/1961 **Genre:** Comedy **MPAA rating:** G

Looking for a silly comedy that's lacking potty humor and adult jokes? You and your kids will find lots to enjoy in this sweet, clever, laugh-out-loud funny movie. The plot centers on a bumbling scientist who invents flying rubber ("flubber") and has all sorts of adventures as a result. Kids may be more familiar with the 1997 remake starring Robin Williams (called *Flubber*), but the original has more heart, even if it may seem a bit dated to kids. Younger kids will go for all of the crazy, bouncy action (there's a good dog in it, too), while aspiring athletes will love the flubber-enhanced basketball game. Content-wise, there's nothing to worry about here. Gather the kids, pop some corn, and enjoy!

The Adventures of Milo and Otis

A lovable pet tale.

on 5+

★★★★★

Director: Masanori Hata **Cast:** Dudley Moore **Running time:** 90 minutes **Theatrical release date:** 8/25/1989 **Genre:** Drama **MPAA rating:** G

Got an animal-obsessed kid? Check out this cute tale of friendship between a frisky kitten and a timid puppy. Kids will love the thrills and the adorable animals; parents will get a kick out of the fact that Dudley Moore voices Milo, Otis, and the narrator. Although this is a sweet coming-of-age movie, there are some scary moments as well: Milo gets swept away in the river current, and Otis fights a bear; Milo throws himself off a cliff and must spend the night alone in the dark. The movie addresses the cyclical nature of life, demonstrating that birth and death are part of the process. And Milo and Otis are sometimes scamps, but it's all in good fun.

Akeelah and the Bee

Inspiring drama about a champion speller.

ON 8+

★★★★

Director: Doug Atchison **Cast:** Keke Palmer, Angela Bassett, Laurence Fishburne **Running time:** 112 minutes **Theatrical release date:** 4/28/2006 **Genre:** Drama **MPAA rating:** PG

Smart kids, unite! This feel-good movie about a dynamic spelling champ will make families feel like the community that rallies around heroine Akeelah: inspired. Especially since she goes through a lot to realize her potential, at first rejecting her talents by showing a lot of attitude and hiding behind some of what one character calls "ghetto" speak (and a little of the "s" word). She also copes with loss, recalling her parents' divorce and the death of a loved one by gun violence. Tension between Akeelah and her mom (Angela Bassett) and Akeelah and her tough-but-supportive coach (Laurence Fishburne) keep you guessing if she's going to triumph.

Aladdin

A magic carpet ride of a movie from Disney.

Director: Ron Clements, John Musker **Cast:** Robin Williams, Scott Weinger, Linda Larkin **Running time:** 90 minutes **Theatrical release date:** 11/25/1992 **Genre:** Animated **MPAA rating:** G

Robin Williams was made to play a giant blue genie. Kids will love every second he's animated on screen, singing and granting wishes to Aladdin, a simple street urchin who wants to impress Princess Jasmine with a fancy new image. Only Jasmine (in the midriff-baring outfits that many parents wish Disney wouldn't peddle to their princess-happy girls) would rather he just be himself. The evil (and scary) Jafar is on to him and sends out his henchmen with big swords, leading to chase scenes aplenty and some tense moments better handled by kids six and up. More than a decade after this was made, we're reminded that this really is "a whole new world"—some negative Middle Eastern stereotypes seem more vivid today than they once were.

Alice in Wonderland

Surreal Disney classic with wild-card characters.

Director: Clyde Geronimi, Wilfred Jackson, Hamilton Luske
Cast: Kathryn Beaumont, Ed Wynn, Richard Hadyn **Running time:** 75 minutes
Theatrical release date: 7/28/1951 **Genre:** Animated **MPAA rating:** G

Kids love wacky characters, and this classic Disney musical has some of the wackiest. A Mad Hatter; a bellowing, slightly scary Queen of Hearts; a frantic, dapper white rabbit; a hookah-puffing caterpillar; and that riddler the Cheshire cat–all straight from the mind of Lewis Carroll, who wrote *Alice's Adventures in Wonderland* in 1865. Adults love this offbeat, dreamy movie, too–and some children of the '60s see it in a more psychedelic light (although even with a hookah pipe there's nothing here to suggest that connection). Alice does plenty of things parents tell kids not to do–going off with strangers, eating and drinking odd things–leading to the tearful song all kids can relate to, "I Give Myself Very Good Advice (But Very Seldom Follow It)."

Amadeus

Great movie. Stupidly R for a naked tush and a bit of hanky-panky.

Director: Milos Forman **Cast:** F. Murray Abraham, Tom Hulce, Elizabeth Berridge
Running time: 160 minutes **Theatrical release date:** 9/19/1984 **Genre:** Drama
MPAA rating: R

This movie would never be rated R today. There's a brief glance of a naked backside right at the beginning, and Amadeus (Tom Hulce) does have a healthy sex drive–but it's mostly talk in this fabulous biopic. Young teens and older will actually really enjoy bad-boy Amadeus and his evil, jealous rival Salieri (F. Murray Abraham). The real Wolfgang Amadeus Mozart wasn't the scruffy, impish "sk8er boi" type depicted here–and there's no real evidence that Salieri engaged in a conspiracy to murder him–but the music is amazing, and so are the stars. Overall, it's a fabulous way to introduce your kids to one of the great figures in history.

American Graffiti

Coming-of-age classic still a must-see for teens.

on 13+

★★★★★

Director: George Lucas **Cast:** Richard Dreyfuss, Ron Howard, Harrison Ford **Running time:** 110 minutes **Theatrical release date:** 8/11/1973 **Genre:** Comedy **MPAA rating:** PG

Parents don't need to worry that this film is dated. George Lucas' 1960s story holds up beautifully. It's the last summer night before college begins, and four friends confront their dreams, fears, and regrets as they drink, eat, talk, and drag race through a small California town. Because it's set in the '60s, there's smoking and loads of drinking. There's also a fistfight, some off-screen gunshots, car mishaps, and some language you might not want your kids using at the dinner table. Teens challenge authority, drink and drive, talk about sex, make out, and, yes, there's the odd shot of the naked backside. But most of all, there's a timeless tale about friendship and growing up.

Angels in the Outfield

Feel-good movie about hope and baseball.

on 7+

★★★★☆

Director: William Dear **Cast:** Danny Glover, Christopher Lloyd, Tony Danza **Running time:** 102 minutes **Theatrical release date:** 7/15/1994 **Genre:** Comedy **MPAA rating:** PG

This uplifting remake of the same-named 1951 classic is a must-see for baseball-loving kids—but even non-sporty types will connect with the inspiring story. Kids will root for Roger to reconnect with his family and for the last-place Angels to win the pennant; parents will enjoy watching big names like Danny Glover, Christopher Lloyd, and Matthew McConaughey. Be aware that there's some mild language, as well as a fight scene with a few punches. While the film is about angels, it's more about faith and love than a particular religious view. The main character and his best friend live in a foster home (which may upset sensitive kids), and there are a few emotionally intense scenes. Use the movie to spark a conversation about hope, faith, and the meaning of family.

Annie

Tale of cute orphan is great for the whole family.

Director: John Huston **Cast:** Aileen Quinn, Albert Finney, Carol Burnett **Running time:** 127 minutes **Theatrical release date:** 6/18/1982 **Genre:** Musical **MPAA rating:** PG

The film adaptation of Little Orphan Annie's story is every bit as delightful as the Broadway musical. The notoriously red-headed, spunky orphan ends up adopted by mega-rich Daddy Warbucks after winning him over with her charm and positive attitude. But drunken Miss Hannigan–played particularly well by Carol Burnett–decides there's money to be made off Annie's good fortune. Disgruntled orphans and moments of peril are peppered throughout the film, but songs like "It's the Hard Knock Life" and "Tomorrow" will have kids crooning in no time. The movie could be used to introduce the concept of adoption or getting along with peers. It's also a great starter musical for starry-eyed kids with a taste for dancing or singing.

Babe

Heartwarming farm tale is touching–and a bit scary.

Cast: Christine Cavanaugh, Miriam Margolyes, Danny Mann **Running time:** 89 minutes **Theatrical release date:** 8/4/1995 **Genre:** Drama **MPAA rating:** PG

The story of this spunky little pig–who seems to have no future but to eat and be eaten–will inspire viewers of all ages. *Babe* is filled from beginning to end with marvelous images: live-action animals who can talk (to each other, not to humans), the never-never land of Hoggett's almost-magical farm, and endless surprising details. But the movie is more than eye candy–it's also full of great messages about making a place for yourself in the world. The harsh reality that farm animals are meant to feed humans may not sit well with some younger viewers, but that's likely to go over the head of youngsters, who will be tantalized by the beauty and fantasy of this wonderful animal world.

Back to the Future

'80s sci-fi time-travel hit offers laughs and romance.

Director: Robert Zemeckis **Cast:** Michael J. Fox, Christopher Lloyd, Lea Thompson **Running time:** 116 minutes **Theatrical release date:** 7/3/1985 **Genre:** Science Fiction **MPAA rating:** PG

This funny, fast-paced '80s favorite is a great adventure for tweens and up. Some of the references are a bit dated now (Tab, anyone?), but stars Michael J. Fox and Christopher Lloyd are as entertaining as ever, the DeLorean time machine is still really cool, and the themes of true love and believing in yourself never get old. Expect some language (the "s" word is said a few memorable times, there's a reference to "reefer," and the bad guys use a few racial slurs) and bullying, as well as an upsetting shooting by a group of Libyan terrorists. It doesn't take up more than three minutes of the story, but it's impossible to ignore. Sex, both wanted and unwanted, is implied, but it's pretty harmless and will go right over a kid's head. The two sequels (the creatively named *Back to the Future Part II* and *Back to the Future Part III*) aren't quite as good, though the Western-themed third entry has its share of fans.

Bambi

Disney's original circle-of-life story.

on 5+ ★★★★★

Director: David Hand **Cast:** Hardie Albright, Stan Alexander, Peter Behn **Running time:** 70 minutes **Theatrical release date:** 8/21/1942 **Genre:** Animated **MPAA rating:** G

This simple, animated coming-of-age tale still works for younger kids (and the young at heart). The relaxed pace and symphonic music might seem odd to kids accustomed to snappy dialogue and splashy song-and-dance numbers, but it's hard to resist the adorable forest creatures and their playful antics. Compared to most of today's animated movies, the violence here is minimal, but it's more realistic than the action-adventure, fantasy, or slapstick kind kids are used to–and so might have a stronger impact. Bambi's mother's death (by a gunshot wound) is only heard, not seen, but her death and subsequent absence are emotionally intense. The movie can be used as a jumping-off point for a "circle of life" conversation.

Barbershop

Charming urban comedy for teens.

Director: Tim Story **Cast:** Ice Cube, Sean Patrick Thomas, Cedric the Entertainer **Running time:** 102 minutes **Theatrical release date:** 9/13/2002 **Genre:** Comedy **MPAA rating:** PG-13

Here's a great pick for your older, edgier kids. This street-smart, hilarious movie has an uplifting message about the importance of community. The lively ensemble cast–including Ice Cube, Cedric the Entertainer, and rapper Eve–will appeal to teens. Know that it's a somewhat racy choice, with talk of adultery, some drug use, and plenty of street language, including the "n" word. Some comments one character makes about early civil rights leaders were very controversial, but since they are objected to by the other people in the movie, it's a great way to spark a conversation with your kids about equality, opportunity, and the African American experience in this country.

DVD note: *On the Special Edition, features include a lot of salty language (the "f" word and "motherf--ker" in "The Final Cut" featurette, "asshole" in interviews, "s--t" in a deleted scene, and all of the above make the Blooper Reel); and you'll find more sexual content in the deleted scenes (pelvic thrusting, and a gun is loaded next to a girl covered by a sheet in bed); "Barber School Interactive Trivia Game" includes the words "syphilis" and "areola."*

Batman Begins

Smart and entertaining, but also very violent.

Director: Christopher Nolan **Cast:** Christian Bale, Michael Caine, Cillian Murphy, **Running time:** 140 minutes **Theatrical release date:** 6/15/2005 **Genre:** Action/Adventure **MPAA rating:** PG-13

Looking for a smart superhero movie for your teens? This gritty blockbuster offers fast action, talented actors (Morgan Freeman and Christian Bale), and the origins of Batman's story, all of which add up to an appealing movie for teens. Expect a good bit of violence (shootings, martial arts violence) that's less cartoonish than what you'd see in the *Spider-Man* or *X-Men* movies, as well as some smoking, drinking, and hallucinogenic drug effects. Batman's parents were murdered, and his quest for revenge is a major theme. There's also some minor profanity, mostly of the "hell" and "damn" variety. Teens and parents can engage in a lively debate about which *Batman* movie is their favorite (and which actor makes the best Batman); this Oscar-nominated entry is widely considered the best.

Beauty and the Beast

You can't judge a beast by his cupboard.

On 5+ ★★★★★

Director: Gary Trousdale, Kirk Wise **Cast:** Paige O'Hara, Robby Benson, Richard White **Running time:** 84 minutes **Theatrical release date:** 11/22/1991 **Genre:** Animated **MPAA rating:** G

This award-winner is a huge hit with ages 5 to 105. It's Disney magic at its best, combining a brisk storytelling pace with stellar music and delightful animation. Nobody is who they seem in this fairy tale. Beast may start out looking scary and ferocious, but he's a love-struck softy in no time. Belle is a bookworm and not the old-fashioned princess type (although she *is* held captive in Beast's castle–that's pretty old-school). And the objects in Beast's enchanted castle are really alive–a teapot gives Belle a sympathetic ear, and a candelabra and feather duster flirt and kiss. Everyone is unpredictable except Gaston, the meathead who ferociously fights Beast (in a scene too intense for younger kids)–he really is the rote scorned-man villain who won't take "no" for an answer (and uses "antlers in all of [his] decorating"). Poor Belle.

Bend It Like Beckham

Superb rendering of a girl's struggle to do what she loves.

Director: Gurinder Chadha **Cast:** Parminder Nagra, Keira Knightley, Jonathan Rhys Meyers **Running time:** 112 minutes **Theatrical release date:** 8/1/2003 **Genre:** Comedy **MPAA rating:** PG-13

Watch this feel-good flick with your soccer-playing teen girls (even though it's really about second-generation Indian families in England striving to maintain traditions that the kids, more British than Indian, find increasingly irrelevant). No matter what your cultural background, the central theme of following your bliss–no matter what the hurdles–is universal. Some of the movie's themes require a bit of perspective and maturity. Jess, the Indian soccer whiz, hides her playing from her family, but she eventually learns that lying about something so important to her is something she can't do. Jess is a clear-thinking, principled girl: She makes it clear that she won't sleep with a guy until she's in a serious relationship, even though some of her acquaintances refer to their own more casual dalliances. A friend comes out to Jess in a very delicate way, and there's a parental misunderstanding about another character's sexual orientation. There's some drinking, but the girls drink responsibly and are of legal age in the UK and Germany, where the scenes take place. This movie is an excellent way to talk with your kids about what they want to do with their lives and how it differs from your agenda for them.

DVD note: *On the Standard Edition, one deleted scene discusses premarital sex and virginity, and includes the word "bitch."*

Big

Wonderful story with some mature material.

on 12+

★★★★☆

Director: Penny Marshall **Cast:** Tom Hanks, Elizabeth Perkins, Robert Loggia **Running time:** 104 minutes **Theatrical release date:** 6/3/1988 **Genre:** Comedy **MPAA rating:** PG

Older tweens who can't wait to grow up may have second thoughts after watching this comedic fantasy, which helped turn Tom Hanks into the megastar he is today. (Or maybe not, since he gets a job playing with toys all day!) Kids will be delighted with set pieces like the classic "Heart and Soul" number Hanks performs with co-star Robert Loggia. Meanwhile, the more mature themes–despite his outward appearance, Hanks' character is a thirteen-year-old who's having sex and dealing with corporate life–won't really make an impression. If you haven't seen *Big* in awhile, you might not remember the occasional strong language (including one "f" word) and frequent smoking (Elizabeth Perkins' character lights up repeatedly). For a girlier take on a similar concept, try *13 Going on 30*.

Billy Elliot

Terrific story of a young boy ballet dancer.

Director: Stephen Daldry **Cast:** Jamie Bell, Julie Walters, Jamie Driven
Running time: 110 minutes **Theatrical release date:** 10/13/2000 **Genre:** Drama
MPAA rating: R

Sometimes the raters get it wrong in reverse. *Billy Elliot*, a hardscrabble story about a boy who wants to follow his dream of being a dancer, received an R rating because of its rough (but appropriate for the characters) language. But the message of working hard against the odds to accomplish a dream is a powerful one for kids. Most teens today can deal with sex talk, a brief glimpse of bare buttocks, homophobic comments, and a transvestite character. Some may be upset by the way that family members treat each other–they're insulting, neglectful, and cruel, and a parent hits a child and threatens another. This is definitely a movie to watch *with* your kids and talk after about what happens when a child's interests go against a parent's prejudices.

The Brave Little Toaster

on 5+
★★★★

Appliances make a suspenseful, incredible journey.

Director: Jerry Rees **Cast:** Deanna Oliver, Jon Lovitz, Phil Hartman
Running time: 90 minutes **Theatrical release date:** 7/10/1987 **Genre:** Animated
MPAA rating: NR

This sure-to-be-favorite movie is an anomaly among Disney's normally upbeat, bright, animated film themes. Not only does it feature inanimate objects–household appliances–as the main characters, but it sustains a palpable sense of suspense throughout the story. Will the characters, abandoned in a cottage by the little boy they refer to as "the master" (voiced by Timothy Day), be able to find him in the big city? Will they even make it there intact, faced as they are with unfriendly terrain, greedy repair-shop parts hunters, and jealous city appliances? Did you ever think you'd care so much about an electric blanket and a toaster? Children younger than five might enjoy the story, but they could get anxious about the characters' fate. Even though we're dealing with appliances being hurt, they're appliances the audience cares about. Families with kids under five might want to watch the 1998 sequel, *The Brave Little Toaster Goes to Mars*, which is lighter and a tad less suspenseful.

Breaking Away

Rousing bicycle race story is a family favorite.

Director: Peter Yates **Cast:** Dennis Christopher, Dennis Quaid, Daniel Stern **Running time:** 100 minutes **Theatrical release date:** 7/20/1979 **Genre:** Comedy **MPAA rating:** PG

Looking for a sports drama that offers more than just thrilling action? Try this Academy Award-winning film about a dedicated teen cyclist who's looking for redemption. Tweens and teens will identify with Dave, who, like most teens, is trying to figure out who he is; parents will appreciate the movie's message about pursuing your dreams through hard work. With solid writing, strong performances, and gorgeous cinematography, there's much more here than you'd expect from an "underdog" movie. Expect some moderate profanity and tense scenes. While no one gets critically injured, there's lots of fighting and some bike-related injuries. Dave pretends to be Italian, and there's some class tension between college students and locals. Even if your kids aren't Lance Armstrong wannabes, they'll find plenty to enjoy and talk about.

Cars

on 5+

★★★★

Pixar comedy is full of four-wheeled fun.

Director: John Lasseter, Joe Ranft **Cast:** Owen Wilson, Bonnie Hunt, Paul Newman **Running time:** 116 minutes **Theatrical release date:** 6/9/2006 **Genre:** Animated **MPAA rating:** G

Car-loving kids are sure to get a kick out of this high-octane comedy. There's not too much here to worry parents, either: The car characters do some pretty raucous racing (careening off walls, trees, and each other), lose their tempers, get into a few mild arguments, and flirt innocently, but overall it's about as safe as playing with Matchbox toys. Kids might hear one or two iffy words ("hell" is about as strong as it gets), but the messages about loyalty, patience, and friendship will come through loud and clear. It's worth noting that, at 116 minutes, *Cars* is on the long side for animation, which means some kids might have trouble paying attention for the whole thing. But if they can, stay tuned for the closing credits—they're some of Pixar's best.

Casablanca

Every kid should see this Bogart classic.

on 10+

★★★★★

Director: Michael Curtiz **Cast:** Humphrey Bogart, Ingrid Bergman, Paul Henreid **Running time:** 102 minutes **Theatrical release date:** 1/23/1943 **Genre:** Classics **MPAA rating:** PG

This classic wartime drama is required viewing for young film lovers. Why? It may be the most famous Hollywood movie of all time and is certainly the most quoted and the most frequently cited as all-time favorite. Although some kids may initially be skeptical, those who give it a chance will be swept away by the romantic story, fine acting, and exotic locales. Then they'll finally understand what all the fuss is about! Know that kids may need some of the political and historical context explained to them, and that characters are in peril. Much of the action takes place in a bar, and Rick drinks when he's unhappy about seeing Ilsa again. Overall, this is a great choice for family movie night.

Chariots of Fire

Brilliant true story of 1924 Olympic footrace.

on 10+

★★★★★

Director: Hugh Hudson **Cast:** Ian Charleson, Ben Cross, Iam Holm **Running time:** 123 minutes **Theatrical release date:** 10/9/1981 **Genre:** Drama **MPAA rating:** PG

This Oscar-winning tale of two athletes competing in the 1924 Olympics will appeal to kids who like sports movies as well as those who just like good stories in general. The races are riveting, and the famous score perfectly accompanies the action. You might warn kids that this movie isn't like the formulaic "underdog" movies they're probably familiar with; *Chariots* is more concerned with the runners' different motivations for competing than blasting stadium anthems like "We Will Rock You." Know that a Jewish athlete deals with prejudice, while a Christian one struggles with the dictates of his religion and the requirements of the sport. There are also tense competition scenes. Families will find lots to talk about, from what inspires athletes to how the world has changed since the time of this movie (which is based on actual events).

A Charlie Brown Christmas

The Peanuts gang in a classic Christmas special.

on 2+

★★★★★

Director: Bill Melendez **Cast:** Peter Robbins, Tracy Stratford, Christopher Shea **Running time:** 25 minutes **Release date:** 12/9/1965 **Genre:** Animated **Rating:** NR

This timeless treasure brims with holiday spirit. Kids love traditions, and this is a great candidate for an annual must-see. The first of the TV specials based on Charles Schultz's long-running comic strip, this just-right-for-little-kids tale sets the standard for those that followed. Simple drawings, a gently meandering story, Schultz's beloved characters, and Vince Guaraldi's lively score combine to make this something the entire family will want to watch every year. The image of the pathetic but endearing Christmas tree, unable to support even one decoration, cleverly parallels the Charlie Brown character. That sad fir springing to life at the end, as Charlie's melancholy dissipates, resonates with young and old alike.

Charlotte's Web

Enchanting take on a beloved children's classic.

on 5+

★★★★★

Director: Gary Winick **Cast:** Julia Roberts, Dakota Fanning, Dominic Scott Kay **Running time:** 97 minutes **Theatrical release date:** 12/15/2006 **Genre:** Drama **MPAA rating:** G

Whether you're new to the story or already adore E.B. White's 1952 Newbery Award-winning book, this film is a special treat. Real-life actors and animals with animated mouths transport the audience into the world of the barnyard without ever doubting its magic. Nurtured by young Fern (Dakota Fanning), runt piglet Wilbur learns the way of the farm, and his new friends–mainly spider Charlotte (voiced by Julia Roberts)–teach him the importance of believing in yourself. While the farmer's plan to kill Wilbur for dinner is referenced, the pivotal (and most potentially upsetting) moment is the death of a central character, which is followed by mourning and recovery by her barnyard friends.

Chicken Run

Fabulous animation from *Wallace and Gromit* creator.

Director: Peter Lord, Nick Park **Cast:** Mel Gibson, Jane Horrocks, Lynn Ferguson **Running time:** 84 minutes **Theatrical release date:** 6/21/2000 **Genre:** Animated **MPAA rating:** G

This poultry-fied *Great Escape* from the creators of *Wallace and Gromit* is a visual treat for kids that's filled with enchanting British humor (some jokes take a few viewings for us Yanks to catch). Mel Gibson voices the American outsider, a circus rooster whom the plucky heroine, Ginger, believes can help the hens escape before it's too late–the farmers are assembling an ominous contraption that can turn them all into pies! Kids under six will likely be too chicken to watch: The nail-biting action sequence in the pie-maker could give the *Indiana Jones* franchise a run for its money.

Chitty Chitty Bang Bang

A car story custom made for kids.

on 6+ ★★★★

Director: Ken Hughes **Cast:** Dick Van Dyke, Sally Ann Howes, Lionel Jeffries **Running time:** 144 minutes **Theatrical release date:** 12/18/1968 **Genre:** Classics **MPAA rating:** G

Kids with strong imaginations are bound to be fascinated by this whimsical tale about a family's adventures in their flying car, which was based on a novel by James Bond creator Ian Fleming and co-scripted by *Charlie and the Chocolate Factory* author Roald Dahl. Dick Van Dyke plays a single inventor/dad who's raising his two kids lovingly, if a bit haphazardly (when the film opens, they're dirty and skipping school). The creepy Child Catcher might scare really young viewers, and there's a scene in which Chitty is pursued (and shot at) by a zeppelin, as well as one in which the Baron comically (and unsuccessfully) tries to do his wife in. And the two-hour plus runtime drags a little near the end. But the songs are awfully catchy, and most kids will be captivated.

A Christmas Story

Wonderful antidote to saccharine holiday stories.

on 8+

★★★★★

Director: Bob Clark **Cast:** Melinda Dillon, Darren McGavin, Peter Billingsley **Running time:** 94 minutes **Theatrical release date:** 11/18/1983 **Genre:** Comedy **MPAA rating:** PG

Santa's sarcastic "ho ho hoooo" as he pushes little Ralphie down the slide with his boot says it all: This hilarious comedy takes holiday cheer and spins it on its elfin ears. It's best for older kids (tweens and up) and nostalgic parents who've known the joys of wishing for and getting the perfect gift (too bad it's a BB gun in this case)—and the agony of suffering through embarrassing gifts like pink bunny pj's. Working toward the big build-up to Christmas, young Ralphie stands up to some bullies in a skirmish that gets a little intense and has his mouth washed out with soap for swearing (the actual word isn't spoken aloud), while a double-dog-dared classmate sticks his tongue to a frozen flag pole (ouch!).

The Chronicles of Narnia: The Lion, the Witch, and the Wardrobe

Timeless classic faithfully rendered.

on 9+

★★★★☆

Director: Andrew Adamson **Cast:** Georgie Henley, Tilda Swinton, William Moseley **Running time:** 143 minutes **Theatrical release date:** 12/9/2005 **Genre:** Fantasy **MPAA rating:** PG

Tweens who already love C.S. Lewis' classic Narnia series will be enchanted by seeing their imaginations come to life in this well-produced adaptation—and newbies will get sucked in right along with them. Expect a fair number of sad, scary, and violent scenes, including a bombing during the Blitz in London, key animal characters' deaths, a tense chase by wolves, cruelty and murder on the part of the evil White Witch, and more. Siblings Lucy, Edmund, Peter, and Susan learn to fight and use weapons (swords, bow, and arrow), wielding them without hesitation during the climactic battle scene, which is fairly intense and includes deaths and grave injuries. While not overt, the movie includes Christian imagery (the lion is a Christlike figure who is martyred and reborn) and allegorical storylines, which could spark some family discussion.

Cinderella

Sweet fairy-tale classic for little princesses.

on 5+

★★★★★

Director: Clyde Geronimi, Wilfred Jackson, Hamilton Luske
Cast: Ilene Woods, Verna Felton, Eleanor Audley **Running time:** 74 minutes
Theatrical release date: 2/15/1950 **Genre:** Animated **MPAA rating:** G

Brought to life by Disney animation, this adaptation of Charles Perrault's fairy tale has become a true classic. With its darling talking animals and magical nature, it's a rags-to-riches princess fantasy that will delight kids. Yes, Cinderella has her share of trials and tribulations (oh, those stepsisters and that evil stepmother!), but the story is all but synonymous with Prince Charming, fairy godmothers, and happily ever after–which isn't the harshest lesson to learn (it's not all that realistic, either, but that's what fairy tales are for!). Cinderella may not be the poster girl for women's rights–waiting to be rescued and putting up with being a slave in her own home–but the point will go over young heads. Bottom line? The music and magic are enchanting and a treat to share with young kids.

Cinema Paradiso

Charming Italian film about friendship, movies.

on 13+

★★★★

Director: Giuseppe Tornatore **Cast:** Philippe Noiret, Marco Leonardi, Enzo Cannavale **Running time:** 155 minutes **Theatrical release date:** 2/23/1990
Genre: Drama **MPAA rating:** PG

This charming tale of friendship and the love of movies is the perfect introduction to foreign films for older tweens and young teens. The bittersweet Italian movie (winner of the 1989 Academy Award for Best Foreign Language Film) is accessible to older kids because the story is simple and straightforward: A young boy develops a close friendship with an older man who teaches him to reach for his dreams. Even the most cynical of teens will find this movie moving. Content-wise, there's little to worry about; a character is badly burned, and there's some on-screen kissing (note: the R-rated director's cut features a bit more explicit sexuality). The film's premise could inspire a discussion about friendship and the role movies play in our lives.

Clueless

Charming, funny take on Jane Austen's *Emma*.

on 14+

★★★★

Director: Amy Heckerling **Cast:** Alicia Silverstone, Paul Rudd, Brittany Murphy **Running time:** 97 minutes **Theatrical release date:** 7/19/1995 **Genre:** Comedy **MPAA rating:** PG-13

Teen girls will, like, *totally* love this bubbly comedy–which happens to be a clever literary adaptation in disguise. Jane Austen's 1816 novel *Emma*, about manners and matchmaking among the English upper class, works just as well within the fashion-conscious halls of a Beverly Hills high school. But despite the nonstop parade of labels, shopping obsessions, makeovers, and slang (mixed in with a few curses, including the "s" word), *Clueless* is packed with heart, smarts, and positive messages about staying true to yourself. Plus, star Alicia Silverstone is adorable (and shaped like a real person!) *and* relatable, motorized closet and all. Note that we say *teens*–this movie is full of edgy material. Expect some scenes of teens drinking and smoking various substances, as well as kissing and talk about sex (Silverstone's character is secure in her virginity but considers giving it up at one point).

DVD note: *On the "Whatever!" Edition, you'll hear a little of the "s" word in the featurettes; the term "hymenally challenged" and virginity in general are brought up in the "Class of '95" featurette; plus actors reminisce about kissing other cast members in "Suck 'n' Blow: A Tutorial" and "Drivers Ed," but it's pretty tame.*

The Color Purple

Inspiring, sentimental tale of survival.

on 14+

★★★★★

Director: Steven Spielberg **Cast:** Danny Glover, Whoopi Goldberg, Oprah Winfrey **Running time:** 154 minutes **Theatrical release date:** 12/18/1985 **Genre:** Drama **MPAA rating:** PG-13

Steven Spielberg's big-screen adaptation of Alice Walker's Pulitzer Prize-winning novel isn't always easy to watch, but it's ultimately a moving, inspiring tale about a woman's journey to independence. The performances are excellent: Whoopi Goldberg earned her first Oscar nomination playing abused wife Celie, and Oprah Winfrey (who made this movie before she was a household name) does memorable work as Sofia. But what really makes this movie a stand-out is the way it deals with some pretty complex issues, including abuse, racism, and sexism. The mature subject matter means that you can expect scenes that deal with sexual abuse, beatings, fistfights, and drinking. But very much on the plus side is the fact that the movie presents strong, nuanced African American characters. This is one of those movies that's bound to kick off some good discussion with teens, so make sure to set aside time to talk after watching.

DVD note: *On the two-disc Special Edition, featurettes discuss child and spousal abuse–physical, emotional, and sexual–as well as homosexuality.*

Crouching Tiger, Hidden Dragon

on 12+
★★★★★

Amazing martial arts fairy tale. Magisterial and magical.

Director: Ang Lee **Cast:** Chow Yun Fat, Michelle Yeoh, Zhang Ziyi
Running time: 120 minutes **Theatrical release date:** 12/22/2000
Genre: Action/Adventure **MPAA rating:** PG-13

If you're going to see one martial arts movie with your older kids, this is the one. It's beautiful to watch, and the subtitles won't bother kids because the movie's all about the magical powers of amazing warriors. Even though most of the battles are more ballet-like than bloody, one character is killed when a blade is hurtled into his forehead. And it's a good vs. evil tale so major characters are killed, and one death could be interpreted as suicide. But the movie has strong female characters who are treated with complete parity and are equal to or superior to the men in judgment and combat–which is a great talking point with your kids. There's brief mild language, but subtitles take the punch out of it.

The Dark Crystal

A fantastic but more intense Muppet adventure.

on 7+
★★★★

Director: Jim Henson, Frank Oz **Cast:** Jim Henson, Kathryn Mullen, Frank Oz **Running time:** 154 minutes **Theatrical release date:** 12/17/1982 **Genre:** Fantasy **MPAA rating:** PG

Dark? Yes!. This Henson puppet creature feature is no *Muppets Take Manhattan*. Instead, it's a dangerous otherworld where sinister forces have taken over, and human-like beings called gelflings are killed off and smaller podlings are rounded up, strapped to chairs with big needles, and drained of their "essence" for decrepit, dinosaur-like skeksis (pretty scary creatures, but also big buffoons). Two of the last gelfings, Jen and Kira, are the last hope (as always) to restore peace and goodness in the world by repairing the dark crystal. Chanting, gentle mystics; long-legged Landstriders; a pushy she-ogre; and their roly-poly pet Fizzgig help them sort out all that destiny stuff. This movie isn't for everyone, and surely not for sensitive little ones under seven, but for the right kid just getting into fantasy books, this will rock their world.

Dead Poets Society

Robin Williams in dramatic role as teacher to troubled boys.

Director: Peter Weir **Cast:** Robin Williams, Ethan Hawke, Robert Sean Leonard **Running time:** 128 minutes **Theatrical release date:** 6/9/1989 **Genre:** Drama **MPAA rating:** PG

Older kids will fall hard for this coming-of-age drama; they'll love the way it challenges them to "carpe diem" (seize the day!) and think for themselves. Parents will like it because the movie celebrates the power of language and may induce a love of reading, poetry, and theater. Teen characters are encouraged to think for themselves and pursue their dreams, and the emotional ending may have them tearing up. Still, parents should know that one of the lead characters commits suicide (off-screen) and that they might want to talk with their kids about how they and their peers handle depression, setbacks, and stresses.

Doctor Dolittle

Animal-friendly, kid-friendly classic.

Director: Richard Fleischer **Cast:** Rex Harrison, Samantha Eggar, Anthony Newley **Running time:** 152 minutes **Theatrical release date:** 12/19/1967 **Genre:** Classics **MPAA rating:** G

Eddie Murphy may have starred in an updated version of this classic in 1998, but no one compares to Rex Harrison when it comes to talking to the animals. This warm, wonderful tale is delightfully wholesome, with lively songs, fuzzy animals, dancing, and cavorting. You can't go wrong. Children younger than five will appreciate the fun and silliness, but they may be impatient with the slowish first half. For older kids, this is nonstop wholesome entertainment that parents can feel good about.

Dr. Seuss' How the Grinch Stole Christmas!

Heartwarming TV special true to Seuss' classic.

on 4+
★★★★★

Director: Chuck Jones, Ben Washam **Cast:** Boris Karloff, June Foray, Thurl Ravenscroft **Running time:** 26 minutes **Theatrical release date:** 12/23/1966 **Genre:** Animated **MPAA rating:** UR

This classic animated retelling of the beloved Theodore Geisel book is true to its roots. It's the day before Christmas, and all the Grinch can think about is how much he hates the entire holiday season–and particularly the Whos in Whoville, who string up lights, hang wreaths, and fill Whoville with hearty holiday happiness. And so begins his plot to stop Christmas from coming. Can the fun and good cheer of the holiday save his shriveled heart? While there's some minor peril and the Grinch's dog, Max, is cartoonishly abused (slammed into a snow drift and run over by a sleigh), there's far more here to recommend than to worry about. The heartwarming holiday story is a great introduction to Dr. Seuss and a nostalgic treat for parents. (Jim Carrey's portrayal of the Grinch in the 2000 live-action version is a sugarplum for older siblings.)

Dr. Strangelove, or: How I Learned to Stop Worrying and Love the Bomb

Classic Kubrick black comedy for smart teens and up.

Director: Stanley Kubrick **Cast:** Peter Sellers, George C. Scott, Sterling Hayden **Running time:** 96 minutes **Theatrical release date:** 1/29/1964 **Genre:** Comedy **MPAA rating:** PG

This black comedy classic will challenge teens who enjoy satire or are looking for something a little edgy. It's definitely not for every taste, but kids with an interest in history or film will consider this a must-see. Know that although it's a comedy, it is about nuclear war, and kids may need some background to understand what was happening during the Cold War years. More important, they may need some preparation to understand the nature of black comedy. Some kids may find the movie very disturbing–particularly the unconventional ending, in which the world is annihilated. Planes are shot down, there's an off-camera suicide, and there are some sexual references. Teens who enjoy it will probably want to check out other Kubrick movies, like *2001: A Space Odyssey*.

Drumline

on 11+

Outstanding cast, great message, strong language.

Director: Charles Stone III **Cast:** Nick Cannon, Zoe Saldana, Orlando Jones **Running time:** 118 minutes **Theatrical release date:** 12/13/2002 **Genre:** Drama **MPAA rating:** PG-13

Devon (Nick Cannon) is an inner-city kid who can really play the drums. But when he wins a full scholarship to college and starts playing in their marching band, he has to learn what it means to be part of something bigger than himself. Set against the background of a big competition sponsored by BET, this story of getting over yourself and finding out what it takes to develop a good character has great messages for tweens and is hip enough for teens. If you have a kid who thinks that simple talent is enough to win, this movie is a must-see for its messages of teamwork, belonging, and how to harness a gift for the good of all. Just keep an ear out for some strong language (the "s" word and more) and a bit of innuendo.

E.T. the Extra-Terrestrial

Touching family classic is still one of the best.

Director: Steven Spielberg **Cast:** Henry Thomas, Dee Wallace, Drew Barrymore **Running time:** 115 minutes **Theatrical release date:** 6/11/1982 **Genre:** Science Fiction **MPAA rating:** PG

This is an outstanding family movie—one of the all-time best. Its themes of loyalty, trust, and caring are both affecting and easy to understand, and Elliot and E.T.'s extraordinary friendship is one of cinema's most enduring. Some scenes of peril and danger may be too intense for very young children (although guns were replaced by walkie-talkies in the newer edition), and a key character's apparent death will be emotional for just about everyone. Brief strong language includes the "s" word and "son of a bitch," there's a bit of squabbling among siblings, and E.T. does get tipsy in one comic scene. But when Elliott's bicycle lifts up into the sky and soars across the moon, all you'll remember is the joy of movie magic done right.

Edward Scissorhands

Dark yet sweet underdog tale for older kids.

on 13+
★★★★

Director: Tim Burton **Cast:** Johnny Depp, Winona Ryder, Dianne Wiest **Running time:** 105 minutes Theatrical release date12/14/1990 **Genre:** Fantasy **MPAA rating:** PG-13

Johnny Depp will be the draw for this offbeat movie. It's the weird, warped Frankenstein story of a lonely, loveless boy who finds friendship in the bosom of suburbia. Lovingly directed by Tim Burton, the film is a darkly sweet (self-) portrait of adolescent angst. We can all relate on some level to Edward's social awkwardness, and Depp's deer-in-the-headlights self-consciousness makes you fall in love with him. The movie has some moments that are best left for older kids—such as when a woman in a lacy bra attempts to seduce Edward. And there are a few moments when his scissor hands do some violent damage in anger and frustration. But this stylish, endearing movie is sure to capture teen hearts and—fair warning—parents', too.

Elf

Peppy holiday favorite for both kids and parents.

on 7+

★★★★

Director: Jon Favreau **Cast:** Will Ferrell, James Caan, Zooey Deschanel **Running time:** 97 minutes **Theatrical release date:** 11/7/2003 **Genre:** Comedy **MPAA rating:** PG

As funny as many of Will Ferrell's characters are, most of them aren't exactly little-kid-friendly. Not so Buddy the Elf, a perky, wide-eyed North Pole misfit who will delight everyone from grade-schoolers on up. Buddy's unfriendly treatment by his birth father (and the fact that his mother died when he was a baby) might upset younger or more sensitive kids, but the ultra-happy ending–and sparkly holiday decorations–should help them bounce back. There's a bit of mild potty humor; a couple of gross-out gags involving burping, barfing, and eating some pretty disgusting things; some mild language ("damn," "hell," and so on); and a scene in which Buddy gets drunk by accident. Parents will get a particular kick out of the movie's homage to the classic Rankin and Bass holiday special *Rudolph the Red-Nosed Reindeer.*

Fantasia

A breathtaking animation feat.

on 5+

★★★★★

Director: James Algar, Samuel Armstrong, Ford Beebe **Cast:** Leopold Stokowski, Deems Taylor, Walt Disney **Running time:** 125 minutes **Theatrical release date:** 11/13/1940 **Genre:** Animated **MPAA rating:** G

Disney's landmark animation showcase is still a classic decades after its release. While some scenes may be too intense for the youngest viewers– "The Rite of Spring" segment features a battle to the death between two dinosaurs, and "Night on Bald Mountain" is filled with ghosts and demons, some of which are quite scary–kids of all ages will get a kick out of the pirouetting animals in "Dance of the Hours" and Mickey battling hordes of brooms in "The Sorcerer's Apprentice." Expect some topless female centaurs and scenes of the drunken wine god Bacchus (and his equally inebriated donkey) in "Pastoral." You might be able to use the movie as a way to introduce kids to classical music and composers.

Ferris Bueller's Day Off

Hilarious comedy classic; language makes it PG-13.

Director: John Hughes **Cast:** Matthew Broderick, Alan Ruck, Jeffrey Jones **Running time:** 102 minutes **Theatrical release date:** 6/11/1986 **Genre:** Comedy **MPAA rating:** PG-13

This is probably the all-time classic playing-hooky movie–and the one that made Matthew Broderick a star. Faking illness, high school student Ferris Bueller is left in bed by his clueless parents to "recover." But once they're gone, he springs to action and, explaining his "seize the day" philosophy to viewers, convinces his hardworking (and thus downcast and depressed) friend Cameron to skip school with him. Chaos naturally ensues. And it does so in side-splitting, defy-all-authority ways. Yes, the language would make your grandmother blush, and most of what Ferris does involves lying, scamming, and showing a general disregard for any and all grownups. But as rebellion movies go, this one's a feel-good charmer.

DVD note: *On the Bueller . . . Bueller Special Edition, expect some mild salty language ("asshole," "dickheads") in the featurettes.*

Fiddler on the Roof

Epic portrait of Jewish life during the Russian Revolution.

Director: Norman Jewison **Cast:** Topol, Norma Crane, Leonard Frey **Running time:** 181 minutes **Theatrical release date:** 11/3/1971 **Genre:** Musical **MPAA rating:** G

This great musical has two faces: One is a boisterous, comic look at rural life in a Ukrainian village, and the other is a serious portrait of the sweeping, tragic changes that the Russian Revolution forced on Russian Jews. The film centers on a humble farming family: Tevye (Palestinian-born actor Topol, ably replacing stage musical lead Zero Mostel) is the milkman of Anatevka and a devout Jew who's desperately attempting to hold onto his faith's traditions in the face of both the rebellious actions of his three marrying-age daughters and the increasingly ominous intimidation of czarist officials. As they sing their way through marriages and pogroms, viewers are swept along through love and history. The musical is best spread over two nights (there's an intermission) and treated as a special mini-series. But it's as marvelous today as it was years ago–a timeless treasure.

Finding Nemo

Sweet father-son tale is perfect family viewing.

on 4+

★★★★★

Director: **Andrew Stanton, Lee Unkrich** Cast: **Albert Brooks, Ellen DeGeneres, Alexander Gould** Running time: **100 minutes** Theatrical release date: **5/30/2003** Genre: **Animated** MPAA rating: **G**

Get out the hankies for Pixar's father-son bonding insta-classic that everyone will love. Protective clownfish dad Marlin, after losing his wife and most of his brood to a big fish (in a quick, subtle opening scene), loses his remaining son, Nemo, to a dentist diver who puts him in the office fish tank. Against all odds, Dad crosses the ocean to find him with the help of the hilariously forgetful Dori (Ellen DeGeneres with blue fins). Along the way they meet some sharks with very big teeth (who try to be friendly but still look scary to preschoolers), get snapped at by seagulls, and run into some ouchie jellyfish (Dori gets a bad sting but bounces back). It's quite an adventure, and quite a family reunion. Sniff sniff.

Fly Away Home

Thrilling, touching adventure for animal lovers.

on 8+

★★★★★

Director: **Carroll Ballard** Cast: **Anna Paquin, Jeff Daniels, Dana Delaney** Running time: **107 minutes** Theatrical release date: **9/13/1997** Genre: **Drama** MPAA rating: **PG**

This gorgeously filmed, moving drama about an unconventional father, his morose teenage daughter, and a gaggle of Canadian geese is full of positive messages about hope and conservation. After Amy (Anna Paquin) loses her mother in a car crash, she's forced to live with her off-the-wall dad Thomas (Jeff Daniels). Their relationship is fraught with a realistic tension that kids–particularly older tweens and young tweensB–will be able to relate to. Things change for the better when Amy adopts sixteen goslings and embarks on a mission to lead them to safety (animal-loving kids will adore the birds' antics).

Expect one use of the "s" word (supposedly demanded by the studio, who wanted the movie to have a PG rating so school-age kids wouldn't dismiss it) and a little other mild language. The director and cinematographer previously worked together on another lovely animal-centric movie, *The Black Stallion*.

Freaky Friday

Mother-daughter switch is fun comedic chaos.

on 8+

★★★★☆

Director: Mark Waters **Cast:** Jamie Lee Curtis, Lindsay Lohan, Mark Harmon **Running time:** 97 minutes **Theatrical release date:** 8/6/2003 **Genre:** Comedy **MPAA rating:** PG

It's the freakiest of Fridays when fifteen-year-old Anna (Lindsay Lohan) literally wakes up in her mother's high-heeled shoes, while mom Tess (Jamie Lee Curtis) finds herself hurrying off to homeroom. Following a run-in with a "magic" fortune cookie, the widowed mother of two and her teen daughter–whose busy lives have created a strain in their relationship–switch bodies and are forced to temporarily live each other's lives. Curtis and Lohan's vibrant performances give new life to this remake (the 1976 original starred Jodi Foster and Barbara Harris). There are some tense family scenes, but overall the movie deals with typical issues of parental control and teen rebellion with a dose of tolerance for both parents and kids. Logic aside, tweens will jump at the chance to see their moms dealing with high school drama–and parents will enjoy the heartwarming hilarity that ensues with the old switcheroo.

Gandhi

Brilliant biography that will engage preteens and up.

Director: Richard Attenborough **Cast:** Ben Kingsley, Candice Bergen, Edward Fox **Running time:** 188 minutes **Theatrical release date:** 12/8/1982 **Genre:** Drama **MPAA rating:** PG

This movie is best broken up over two nights (an intermission is built in). Weighing in at three-plus hours, Richard Attenborough's amazing biography of the peaceful leader is a must-see for families with an interest in history or civil rights. Don't worry–your kids (and you) will be so engaged that they'll think of it as a mini-series treat. It's worth noting that even though Gandhi (Ben Kingsley) advocated nonviolence, the movie begins with his assassination and shows brutal beatings and a violent depiction of a shooting massacre. That said, this movie provides a brilliant way to learn about history and the spiritual principles of nonviolence, tolerance, and self-sacrifice.

Ghostbusters

Paranormal fun for the whole family.

on 10+
★★★★☆

Director: Ivan Reitman **Cast:** Bill Murray, Dan Aykroyd, Harold Ramis **Running time:** 105 minutes **Theatrical release date:** 6/8/1984 **Genre:** Comedy **MPAA rating:** PG

"Who you gonna call?" How about ages eight and up who like ghost stories and silly comedy all mashed together? Comedy greats Bill Murray and Dan Aykroyd fight a wave of paranormal mayhem in NYC with fiery lasers and sharp wit (laced with some occasional strong language). When Murray's new love interest is possessed by a being from another dimension (suddenly giving off plenty of sexual energy), the 'busting team steps in to save the day. While there are some scary ghosts–especially in the NY Public Library–a bawdy scene or two (Aykroyd's pants get unzipped by a ghost), and some out-there paranormal concepts, nothing is taken too seriously except the movie's New York City pride. Families will find more of the same in the sequel, *Ghostbusters II*, along with a walking Statue of Liberty.

Goldfinger

Thrilling action comedy may be the best Bond.

on 14+

★★★★☆

Director: Guy Hamilton **Cast:** Sean Connery, Honor Blackman, Gert Frobe **Running time:** 112 minutes **Theatrical release date:** 1/9/1965 **Genre:** Action/Adventure **MPAA rating:** PG

If you and your teens are going to sit down together and watch just one James Bond movie, this is it. Original (and arguably best) 007 Sean Connery plays up the super spy's cheeky side for the first time, setting up the mix of action and humor that would mark the franchise going forward. Speaking of action, there's plenty here, including the requisite deaths, explosions, car chases, gun battles, and fight scenes. And, as always, James drinks his shaken martinis like they're water and puts plenty of moves on the ladies (one of cinema's most iconic images–a naked woman covered in gold body paint–comes from this movie). While many of the bad guys are Japanese men (which means that all of the movie's Japanese characters appear to be evil), there's no verbal stereotyping or use of racial slurs. Overall, a fun choice for a family movie night.

DVD note: *On the Ultimate Edition, extras in-clude more sexy female silhouettes (screen art) and portraits (image gallery), plus featurettes discuss the role of sexual innuendo in the character of "Pussy Galore," and the word "bitch" is used in an interview.*

The Goonies

A classic '80s action-fantasy–tweens will love!

on 10+

★★★★☆

Director: Richard Donner **Cast:** Sean Astin, Corey Feldman, Josh Brolin **Running time:** 114 minutes **Theatrical release date:** 6/7/1985 **Genre:** Action/Adventure **MPAA rating:** PG

Goonies never say die! Take away all of the swashbuckling adventure (not that you'd want to), and this is the heartwarming message that runs through this Steven Spielberg-produced '80s tween classic: Persistence, loyalty, and friendship are life's real treasures. But back to the adventure... Led by Mikey (Sean Astin), a motley crew of misfit kids sets out to find hidden pirate booty so they can save their neighborhood from demolition. They encounter plenty of scary obstacles–including lots of skeletons and pursuit by a gang of real-life villains–along the way, but most of it is just the kind of seat-edge tension kids love. And, in a nice twist, a character who seems menacing at first turns out to be a strong ally. Expect some standard "movie kid" typecasting (i.e., the geek, the smart aleck, the cheerleader, the chubby guy), a few innuendo-based jokes, and a smattering of bad words (but if you were being chased by the Fratellis, you'd swear, too!).

Gone with the Wind

We know it, we love it, even sixty-plus years later.

on 10+

★★★★★

Director: Victor Fleming **Cast:** Clark Gable, Vivien Leigh, Leslie Howard **Running time:** 238 minutes **Theatrical release date:** 1/17/1939 **Genre:** Classics **MPAA rating:** G

Frankly, my dear, there's a reason we all still give a damn about this epic, Oscar-winning adaptation of Margaret Mitchell's Civil War novel. Kids may need some encouragement to sit down for all four hours of Scarlett O'Hara's trials and tribulations, but once Vivien Leigh bats her eyes and they're hooked, they'll be in it for the long haul. War scenes don't get too violent, though the burning of Atlanta is still frightening, and the wide-angle shot of the thousands of wounded soldiers is sobering. There are some sad and unexpected deaths, and forced sex is implied in one scene (on screen, there's nothing racier than a few kisses). Expect to have a discussion about slavery and stereotypes–the ones here reflect both the antebellum South and the 1930s, when the movie was made.

DVD note: *On the four-disc Collector's Edition: The featurette "The Making of a Legend: Gone with the Wind" discusses the swirl of racial tension surrounding the film; uses the "n" word and "negroes"; and mentions the scandal over the use of the word "damn." The historical film "The Old South" (1940) includes some imagery and dialogue related to the practice of slavery that would be considered racially insensitive today. The featurette "Scarlett and Beyond" discusses adultery, miscarriage, manic depression, shock treatment, and death.*

Grease

Musical phenomenon is great fun but racy.

on 13+

★★★★☆

Director: Randal Kleiser **Cast:** John Travolta, Olivia Newton-John, Stockard Channing **Running time:** 110 minutes **Theatrical release date:** 6/26/1978 **Genre:** Musical **MPAA rating:** PG

Grease is definitely the word when it comes to fun, slumber party-friendly musicals for teens. Boasting classic songs ("Summer Nights," "You're the One That I Want") and one of John Travolta's most iconic performances, this Broadway adaptation is lots of fun–though it's probably a *little* racier than you remember. Rizzo (Stockard Channing) dances in her underwear during "Sandra Dee" (mocking Sandy's virginity in the process) and later has a pregnancy scare (a broken condom is mentioned). Teen characters smoke and drink, a few naked behinds pop up in mooning scenes, the T-Birds are quick to express their appreciation of female anatomy, and "Greased Lightnin'" is chock full of innuendo . . . but it will likely fly over kids' heads. Sandy and Danny's attempts to change to make each other happy could prompt a good talk about peer pressure and conformity.

Groundhog Day

A witty, sarcastic take on redemption.

on 10+

★★★★★

Director: Harold Ramis **Cast:** Bill Murray, Andie MacDowell, Chris Elliott **Running time:** 101 minutes **Theatrical release date:** 2/12/1993 **Genre:** Comedy **MPAA rating:** PG

Here's evidence that you can become a better, happier, fulfilled person in just one day–well, a really long day that Bill Murray's weatherman character lives over and over anyway. The movie's wonderful message about life, love, and the choices we make is delivered with plenty of humor. You can't help rooting for Murray's sarcastic pessimist as he fumbles through February 2. Sometimes he makes really bad choices–including killing himself repeatedly and waking up the next day saying he's "invincible," and studying women so he can trick them into bed (he gets kissed a little on-screen and slapped a lot). And sometimes he makes great choices, like giving a homeless man he knows will die that day his last warm meal. His tough lessons and the love story at the movie's heart make this a great choice for tweens.

A Hard Day's Night

Beatles classic holds up as fabulously as the Fab Four.

Director: Richard Lester **Cast:** John Lennon, Paul McCartney, George Harrison
Running time: 87 minutes **Theatrical release date:** 8/11/1964 **Genre:** Musical
MPAA rating: G

What a great way to introduce your kids to the Beatles–or just enjoy their glory days together as a family. Join the boys as they present a funny, fictional day-in-the-life, complete with a character who plays Paul's naughty grandfather. Sing along with the soundtrack, which includes "Can't Buy Me Love," "I Should Have Known Better," and "And I Love Her." Warm and witty, this movie holds up as well as the music.

Harry Potter and the Sorcerer's Stone

First Potter movie is a big-budget magical ride.

on 7+
★★★★★

Director: Chris Columbus **Cast:** Daniel Radcliffe, Emma Watson, Rupert Grint
Running time: 152 minutes **Theatrical release date:** 11/16/2001 **Genre:** Fantasy
MPAA rating: PG

Presto, change-o! J.K. Rowling's big bestsellers are also big-budget movies, and they're big fun, too. No, nothing beats the books, but the movies have that same all-ages appeal and open up a fantastic magical world where owls deliver the mail, portraits talk, and charms class is about spells, not manners. Like the books, they start out with seven-year-old scares and get heavier, denser, and more mature. The first (*Sorcerer's Stone*) finds eleven-year-old wizards facing a three-headed dog, an ominous hooded figure in the Forbidden Forest, and a nasty troll in the girls' bathroom. It also discusses how Harry's parents died and shows a character turn to dust. The second (*Chamber of Secrets*, for 8+) offers up a really scary giant snake. By the fourth (*Goblet of Fire*, 10+), Harry is tortured and in some serious mortal danger–and teen wizards talk about all that kissing stuff.

Holes

Great movie respects its audience's intelligence.

on 10+

★★★★

Director: Andrew Davis **Cast:** Shia LaBeouf, Jon Voight, Sigourney Weaver **Running time:** 117 minutes Release date: 4/18/2003 **Genre:** Drama **MPAA rating:** PG

Shia LaBeouf got his movie-star start in this terrific movie adapted from Louis Sachar's bestselling book. When Stanley Yelnats (LaBeouf) is sent to Camp Green Lake–a juvenile facility for boys–for supposedly stealing a pair of sneakers, he joins a cast of young men who each have different stories and issues. The boys are sentenced to digging one hole a day, supposedly to build their characters. But quality of character *really* comes into play in Stanley's friendship with mute Zero. At once a fable and a coming-of-age story, *Holes* deals frankly with some very serious issues, including racism, injustice, and the sometimes-tragic consequences of poor choices. The boys at Green Lake are treated very badly and can be pretty brutal to each other. There's a suicide, some interracial relationships, and language that's on the strong side for a movie directed at middle-schoolers. That said, there's plenty of payoff in the strong messages about friendship, tolerance, and the plain old value of being a good person who keeps promises.

Home Alone

Slapstick family comedy is a modern holiday classic.

Director: Chris Columbus **Cast:** Macaulay Culkin, Joe Pesci, Daniel Stern **Running time:** 103 minutes Release date: 11/16/1990 **Genre:** Comedy **MPAA rating:** PG

Sick of saccharine-sweet holiday movies? You and your kids should check out this silly-but-charming comedy about a young boy left behind at Christmas. Kids will get a kick out of Macaulay Culkin's manic performance and all the pratfalls and slapstick humor. The plot requires some major suspension of disbelief: A family accidentally leaves home without their son, who gets into all sorts of mischief and foils the plans of some stupid bandits. But somehow it still works, maybe because Culkin is just so cute. Expect lots of slapstick violence: Characters fall down stairs, get hit with blunt objects, step on nails and glass, get burned, and more. And younger kids might be frightened about the idea of being left behind. But bottom line? This is a modern holiday classic.

Homeward Bound: The Incredible Journey

This adventurous animal tale will have kids riveted.

on 5+

★★★★

Director: Duwayne Dunham **Cast:** Michael J. Fox, Sally Field, Don Ameche **Running time:** 84 minutes **Theatrical release date:** 2/3/1993 **Genre:** Action/ Adventure **MPAA rating:** G

This fast-moving live-action animal adventure will keep kids on the edge of their seats. And with its lush scenery, wisecracking characters, and moving story, this is one kiddie flick that holds up well through repeat viewings. Although kids under five will enjoy the animals, they probably won't follow the story–but those in the target audience (ages five to eight) will adore the talking critters, get what's happening, *and* enjoy the irreverent humor and abundance of attitude. Plus, there are great messages about the importance of family and perseverance. Shadow, Chance, and Sassy do end up in a few perilous situations, and there's a fight, but it all ends up OK. After watching, talk to your kids about what to do if they get separated from you–striking out on a cross-country trip *isn't* their best bet!

Hoop Dreams

Stunning documentary, great family viewing with older kids.

Director: Steve James **Cast:** William Gates, Arthur Agee, Emma Gates
Running time: 170 minutes **Theatrical release date:** 10/14/1994
Genre: Documentary **MPAA rating:** PG-13

If your teens think documentaries are boring, here's the perfect pick to change their minds. This gripping (albeit long) movie follows the trials and tribulations of two young African American basketball standouts from inner-city Chicago. Older kids will relate to William and Arthur's struggles as they try to overcome extremely limited opportunities, potentially fatal temptations, and overwhelmingly poor odds to get basketball scholarships and a ticket to the NBA. There's some strong language, some discussion about both sexuality and drug use (as well as the accompanying consequences), and consumerism in the form of basketball shoes and athletic gear. The young men deal with parental separation and divorce, extreme poverty, sport-related injuries, and urban blight and violence; all of the above make for great conversation starters.

DVD note: *On the Criterion Collection Edition, a series of Siskel and Ebert segments that briefly mention drugs, guns, and violence also discuss the role of race and class in professional sports, as well as the controversy surrounding the film's noticeable absence from the 1994 Oscars (racism is strongly implied).*

Hoosiers

A tale of heroic sportsmanship.

Director: David Anspaugh **Cast:** Gene Hackman, Barbara Hershey, Dennis Hopper **Running time:** 114 minutes **Theatrical release date:** 11/14/1986 **Genre:** Drama **MPAA rating:** PG

This stirring sports drama features exciting basketball action and good life lessons, making it a wonderful choice for tweens and teens. Kids will relate to the high school players and become emotionally invested in the small-town team, and parents will enjoy seeing Gene Hackman (as the dogged basketball coach in search of redemption) and Dennis Hopper in some of their best roles. The movie occasionally succumbs to sports-movie clichés, but it's still one of the most inspiring ones around. Expect some mild profanity and sports melees; the movie also deals with alcoholism. The lessons about teamwork, discipline, and second chances can serve as fodder for many great conversations after the credits roll.

Howl's Moving Castle

Charming Miyazaki fairy tale appeals to boys and girls equally.

Director: Hayao Miyazaki, Rick Dempsey, Pete Docter **Cast:** Jean Simmons, Christian Bale, Lauren Bacall **Running time:** 119 minutes **Theatrical release date:** 6/10/2005 **Genre:** Animated **MPAA rating:** PG

This marvelous movie comes from the same animation genius who brought us *My Neighbor Totoro* and *Spirited Away*. It's a story of a young handsome wizard (voiced by Christian Bale), a young girl cursed to look like an old woman (Emily Mortimer), and a fire demon (Billy Crystal). The movie does have a few mildly scary figures (featureless blob-men, wraithlike wizards, explosions, and war scenes) and a couple of dark night scenes. But its primary imagery is magical and whimsical, including the rather charming titular castle, which clatters and wheezes, walking on mechanical legs. At once a condemnation of war and a celebration of love, this movie will appeal to both boys and girls and will be watched over and over again. (Parents: we bet you, like your kids, will be enchanted enough to see it multiple times.)

The Iron Giant

A director's cut re-release of a wonderful family movie.

Director: Brad Bird **Cast:** Eli Marienthal, Vin Diesel, Jennifer Aniston **Running time:** 86 minutes **Theatrical release date:** 8/6/1999 **Genre:** Animated **MPAA rating:** PG

Your younger kids will love this story about a boy who befriends an enormous robot from outer space. It's told with so much humor and heart that it becomes utterly winning in its own right, as well as one of the best family movies around. Parents should know that there are some tense moments that may be frightening to young children, as well as a bit of potty humor–remind kids that it's *not* funny to feed someone a laxative disguised as chocolate. The movie provides a lot of good discussion topics, including the role of violence and guns (the robot is very upset when a deer is killed by hunters, and it automatically shoots back when it sees a toy gun).

The Indian in the Cupboard

Classic, heartwarming fantasy will rivet kids.

on 6+
★★★★★

Director: Frank Oz **Cast:** Hal Scardino, Litefoot, Lindsay Crouse **Running time:** 96 minutes **Theatrical release date:** 7/14/1995 **Genre:** Fantasy **MPAA rating:** PG

In this film adaptation of Lynne Reid Banks' popular book (a perennial summer reading list pick), a young boy named Omri (Hal Scardino) receives a magical cupboard and key that bring to life an eighteenth-century Iroquois warrior named Little Bear (Litefoot) who's all of three inches tall. Watching the movie (even though it's missing some of the book's characters) is like visiting an old, dear friend. Your kids will love the friendship between Omri and Little Bear; it's a journey of self-discovery and growth. The warrior is the film's main strength, as he teaches Omri about the pain of personal loss and the responsibility that is part of growing up. The effects are marvelous, the story impeccable, and the adaptation, while not always totally faithful, is skillful and true to the spirit of the book.

The Incredibles

Incredible! But action is too much for youngest kids.

Director: Brad Bird **Cast:** Craig T. Nelson, Holly Hunter, Jason Lee **Running time:** 115 minutes **Theatrical release date:** 11/5/2004 **Genre:** Animated **MPAA rating:** PG

With Pixar-perfect animation, super storytelling, brilliant action sequences, and all-ages humor, there's something for everyone here. The Incredibles family sports super-strength, -stretch, -speed, and powerful force fields–and is letting all these superpowers go to waste living a normal life in the 'burbs. That is, until vengeful, whiny villain Syndrome unveils his sinister plot of world domination/destruction and lures the Incredibles to his secret tropical island. While the family works together to fight Syndrome's techno killing machines, they do some serious bonding, too. With the intense action and cartoon peril, a reference to suicide, and some smoking by hilariously bossy designer Edna Mode, families with kids over seven will want to bond over this one, too.

It's a Wonderful Life

This classic delivers warmth all year long.

on 9+
★★★★★

Director: Frank Capra **Cast:** James Stewart, Donna Reed, Lionel Barrymore **Running time:** 130 minutes **Theatrical release date:** 1/7/1947 **Genre:** Drama **MPAA rating:** UR

This perennial holiday favorite remains a great pick for families with tweens and up. Frank Capra's bittersweet, heartwarming movie about a man who comes to realize the value of his own life is delightful; some kids may be turned off by the old-fashioned feel, but those who give it a chance will understand why it's one of the most famous and well-loved movies around. Of course, it's not all sweetness and light: George feels like a failure and contemplates suicide, and there's some minor violence in the form of gunshots and a fistfight. George's younger brother chases their African American maid, trying to grab her butt. But the movie conveys an important message about the value of an individual life and how one person's actions affect others; it's a perfect entry into a discussion about how we can all make a difference.

James and the Giant Peach

Fabulous adaptation of Roald Dahl's classic book.

on 7+

★★★★

Director: Henry Selick **Cast:** Paul Terry, Simon Callow, Richard Dreyfuss **Running time:** 79 minutes **Theatrical release date:** 4/12/1996 **Genre:** Animated **MPAA rating:** PG

Combining stop-motion animation and real-life action, this is a quirky—but faithful—adaptation of one of the most beloved children's books. The live action revolves around James, whose idyllic life with his parents is cut short by a charging rhino. James suddenly finds himself bunking in the attic of his aunts' home (with Aunt Spiker played delightfully dastardly by Joanna Lumley of *Absolutely Fabulous*). He's a servant in their home, and the two women threaten that the rhino which killed his parents will return for him if he disobeys them (read: acts like a child). They also threaten to beat him regularly. Some of these scenes could scare little kids. But once the animation sets in—thanks to a magical glow worm that turns a peach into a giant escape vessel complete with fabulous insect characters—the movie sails, with James making his way to freedom across a sea fraught with shark creature perils that might be the tiniest bit scary to kids (but in a delightful way).

The Karate Kid

A classic coming-of-age story that remains fresh.

on 9+

★★★★

Director: John G. Avildsen **Cast:** Ralph Macchio, Pat Morita, Elisabeth Shue **Running time:** 126 minutes **Theatrical release date:** 6/22/1984 **Genre:** Drama **MPAA rating:** PG

Tweens will be cheering for Daniel LaRusso (Ralph Macchio) as he learns to "wax on, wax off" in this inspiring coming-of-age drama. Freshly arrived in Southern California from New Jersey, teenage Daniel has a hard time adjusting to his new surroundings, especially after he runs afoul of bullies from the local karate school. Enter maintenance man Mr. Miyagi (Oscar-nominated Pat Morita), who becomes the boy's Yoda-like mentor. He agrees to teach Daniel karate—albeit in a very unconventional way. In the process, Daniel learns patience, understanding, empathy, and more. Expect a smattering of swearing, one instance of drug use, some fairly intense fight scenes. But without hitting kids over the head with "lessons," *Karate Kid* conveys some very important messages about believing in yourself and finding balance in your life, too. It's a pity none of the sequels (*The Karate Kid, Part II*; *The Karate Kid, Part III*; and *The Next Karate Kid*) are as good.

Lady and the Tramp

Classic Disney dogs paw their way into kids' hearts.

Director: Clyde Geronimi, Wilfred Jackson, Hamilton Luske **Cast:** Barbara Luddy, Larry Roberts, Peggy Lee **Running time:** 76 minutes **Theatrical release date:** 6/22/1955 **Genre:** Animated **MPAA rating:** G

Animal lovers will adore these Disney dogs. Pampered pooch Lady is adjusting to the addition of a baby to her household: Less attention from her owners and a run-in with cat-loving Aunt Sarah–who winds up putting a muzzle on Lady–is more than she can bear. Hurt and humiliated, she runs away; during her aimless roam, she meets streetwise mutt Tramp. Friendship–and shy romance–ensues, but not without a few harried trips to the pound and a quarrel with Aunt Sarah's Siamese cats.C Moments of peril peppered throughout the movie (there's a run-in with the dog-catcher, and a rat goes after the baby) create just enough suspense for a five-year-old. This charming '50s classic has memorable music and will appeal to the whole family.

The Land Before Time

Baby dinosaur buddy flick that started the series.

on 4+

★★★★

Director: Don Bluth **Cast:** Gabriel Damon, Candace Hutson, Judith Barsi **Running time:** 70 minutes **Theatrical release date:** 11/18/1988 **Genre:** Animated **MPAA rating:** G

The Land before Time is a very simple story, nicely animated, that both gives kids some perky characters to follow and shows them the kind of earth the dinosaurs roamed. Kids see how changes in the earth's climate forced dinosaurs to roam long distances to find food and how earthquakes, volcanoes, and even other dinosaurs made survival difficult (which is important, since main character Littlefoot is the only hope for future generations of longnecks). Apart from the fact-based content, the movie conveys lessons of friendship and cooperation that kids will relate to. All of that said, this series has *many* sequels that are really rough for parents to sit through more than once, so be warned: Your kids will want to watch repeatedly!

Lawrence of Arabia

Mature teens will appreciate this gripping epic.

on 13+

★★★★★

Director: David Lean **Cast:** Peter O'Toole, Alec Guinness, Anthony Quinn **Running time:** 216 minutes **Theatrical release date:** 1/30/1963 **Genre:** Classics **MPAA rating:** PG

This gorgeously filmed classic will appeal to teen film buffs and those with an interest in history. It might be a tough sell for some kids because of its length (at almost four hours we recommend breaking this up into three or four mini-series segments) and complexity (the tale of an enigmatic British hero from WWI requires some historical background), but it won't take long before your teens are sucked in by the cinematic magic. This epic is a masterpiece of direction, photography, and acting, especially from Peter O'Toole. Kids may have some questions about the historical context, (yes, it's based on history) and there's some brutal war violence. Lawrence is raped by Turkish captors in one scene, although it's not immediately obvious what's going on. The movie may lead to a discussion of war, leadership, and history.

A League of Their Own

Terrific tweens-and-up story of women's baseball.

on 10+

★★★★

Director: Penny Marshall **Cast:** Geena Davis, Tom Hanks, Madonna **Running time:** 124 minutes **Theatrical release date:** 7/01/1992 **Genre:** Comedy **MPAA rating:** PG

Any movie in which Tom Hanks plays a drunk jerk surely stands out. Here he's the reluctant baseball coach for a women's wartime league. This tender-hearted tale of camaraderie finds strong women actresses in the lead: Geena Davis, Rosie O'Donnell, and Madonna (nicknamed "All-the-Way Mae" here for more than one reason–it's the movie's clearest allusion to hanky panky on the road). It's fun to watch as the ladies throw their fast balls right through the gender stereotypes of the day. The coach's drinking and some wartime sadness (one player hears that her husband has died), make this best suited for ages ten and up.

The Lion King

Disney's tuneful king-of-the-beasts blockbuster.

on 5+

★★★★

Director: Roger Allers, Rob Minkoff **Cast:** Jonathan Taylor Thomas, Matthew Broderick, James Earl Jones **Running time:** 89 minutes **Theatrical release date:** 6/24/1994 **Genre:** Animated **MPAA rating:** G

One of Disney's biggest hits, *The Lion King* has echoes of Shakespeare, bringing to mind the plots of both *Hamlet* and *Richard III*. Of course, kids won't know–or care–about that; they'll just be enthralled by the memorable songs ("Hakuna Matata," "I Just Can't Wait to Be King," "Circle of Life") and great characters (supporting duo Timon and Pumbaa are always kid favorites). The scene in which cub Simba's father, Mufasa, is trampled to death, is both sad and genuinely scary. And some of the fights between animals later in the movie can be frightening as well. But the lesson Simba learns–that you have to stand up to your problems instead of running away from them–is a solid one. Just be prepared to buy the soundtrack after your kids get hooked on "Hakuna Matata". . .

The Little Mermaid

A superbly entertaining animated musical.

on 6+

★★★★★

Director: Ron Clements, John Musker **Cast:** Jodi Benson, Pat Carroll, Samuel E. Wright **Running time:** 83 minutes **Theatrical release date:** 11/17/1989 **Genre:** Animated **MPAA rating:** G

Three days! That's all the mermaid Ariel has when she trades her beautiful singing voice for legs to get Prince Eric to (cue "la la la" frogs) "kiss the girl." No kiss, and she'll be a slave of sea witch Ursula forever. This Hans Christian Andersen fairy-tale adaptation combines qualities of the best Disney movies: a very catchy soundtrack (and a Calypso-singing crab), a plucky heroine (though her only goal seems to be the prince), a despicable villainess, and fast-paced, exciting storytelling. Kids under five may not be ready for the scary sea witch, a rather bloodthirsty French chef, or the climatic final battle scene, but everyone else in the family will be under Ariel's spell.

A Little Princess

Wonderful movie of a lonely girl's triumph.

on 7+

★★★★☆

Director: Alfonso Cuaron **Cast:** Liesel Matthews, Eleanor Bron, Liam Cunningham **Running time:** 97 minutes **Theatrical release date:** 5/10/1995 **Genre:** Fantasy **MPAA rating:** G

Based on the book by Frances Hodgson Burnett, Alfonso Cuaron's adaptation has that combination of magic, drama, boarding-school bullies, and a resilient orphan that probably made him a shoe-in for the job of directing a Harry Potter movie a few years later. Here the heroine is Sara Crewe, a wealthy, motherless girl whose father leaves her in a boarding school when he goes off to fight in the war. When he goes missing, the cruel headmistress puts Sara to work as a maid. Kids will love Sara and her insistence that she's a princess–and that all girls are, no matter what. As she mourns her father, her captivating storytelling helps her cope. While the movie's ending is happier than the book's, the depiction of war (with dead bodies shown in trenches), hardship, loss, and one scary escape make this better choice for ages seven and up.

Little Women

Alcott adaptation tugs at your heartstrings.

Director: Gillian Armstrong **Cast:** Winona Ryder, Kirsten Dunst, Susan Sarandon **Running time:** 115 minutes **Theatrical release date:** 12/21/1994 **Genre:** Drama **MPAA rating:** PG

Moms with tween daughters couldn't do much better than this for a girls' movie night. Louisa May Alcott's classic Civil War-era novel translates beautifully to the screen, with Susan Sarandon at her most inspiring as Marmee, mother hen to March sisters Meg, Jo, Beth, and Amy. The dramas of their daily lives–friendships, romances, parties, sibling spats–may be small (by movie standards, anyway), but they're still very affecting. Prepare to break out the tissues when a main character dies prematurely, but other than that, there's not much to worry about here. If your kids have read the book, talk about how well they think the movie lives up to Alcott's words. Or, for another take on the story, try the 1949 version with Elizabeth Taylor or the 1933 version with Katharine Hepburn.

The Lord of the Rings: The Fellowship of the Ring

on 12+
★★★★★

Fabulous, but also violent and scary.

Director: Peter Jackson **Cast:** Elijah Wood, Sean Astin, Ian McKellen **Running time:** 178 minutes **Theatrical release date:** 12/19/2001 **Genre:** Fantasy **MPAA rating:** PG-13

This movie (and the two others that make up the *Lord of the Rings* trilogy) is that once-in-a-generation, not-since-*Star Wars* transcendent reminder of why we tell stories, why we have imagination, and why we must go on quests to test our spirits and heal the world. That said, the creatures are scary, the battles quite bloody, and the main characters are always one step away from death and destruction. Families who watch this movie might want to talk about why only Frodo seems immune to the ring's power to corrupt even honorable, wise, and powerful people and the notion that "even the smallest person can change the course of the earth." Ask your kids: If they were going to form a fellowship for a grand quest, whom would they want to be in it? (Then hope they answer "you"!)

Mad Hot Ballroom

Dance documentary hits all the right beats.

on 8+
★★★★★

Director: Marilyn Agrelo **Cast:** Elijah Yomaira Reynoso, Michael Vaccaro, Emma Biegacki **Running time:** 105 minutes **Theatrical release date:** 5/13/2005 **Genre:** Documentary **MPAA rating:** PG

If your tweens' toes aren't tapping by the time the credits roll on this heartwarming documentary, you might want to check their pulse. Filmmaker Marilyn Agrelo follows fifth grade students from three New York City public schools as they participate in the city's competitive ballroom dancing program, learning to merengue, tango, rumba, and more. At the same time, they're navigating the realities of urban life, from absent parents to street violence. Nothing graphic is ever shown, but watching ten-year-olds talk about such mature topics so matter-of-factly can be sobering. But the energetic dance footage will have you and your kids up and cheering, especially during the final competition.

March of the Penguins

***The* penguin movie. A stunning, loving documentary.**

Director: Luc Jacquet **Cast:** Morgan Freeman **Running time:** 85 minutes **Theatrical release date:** 7/22/2005 **Genre:** Documentary **MPAA rating:** G

Kids love penguins. But don't settle for animated imitations: Sit back and enjoy this amazing documentary with your whole family. Morgan Freeman narrates as the penguins make their annual march from the Antarctic shore to their breeding grounds and back. You might prepare your little ones that some penguins do die along the way, others freeze during the long winter as they huddle to protect pregnant females and then eggs and babies, and still others are killed by predators. But you can talk to your children about the circle of life and the laws of nature. Kids are very sensitive but very understanding, too. They'll take their cues from your reactions.

Mary Poppins

World's coolest nanny celebrates family and fun.

on 6+

★★★★★

Director: Robert Stevenson **Cast:** Julie Andrews, Dick Van Dyke, David Tomlinson **Running time:** 139 minutes **Theatrical release date:** 8/29/1964 **Genre:** Musical **MPAA rating:** G

In Julie Andrews' first movie (and first Oscar win), she not only commands the Banks household as their no-nonsense nanny, but commands the screen as she cleans out the nursery in a snap, pops in and out of sidewalk drawings, and dances a rooftop jig with a gaggle of chimney sweeps. And, oh, that voice! Is there anything she can't do? Well, she can't stay for long, so she has to teach this distant British family to cherish one another–a wonderful message for families to absorb while watching together. The youngest Poppins fans may be scared when Jane and Michael get lost in London–or when they meet the creepy old bank president or the quirky, sea-loving neighbors who set off canons on their roof–but for the rest they'll laugh "loud and long and clear."

Mean Girls

Mature but often-hilarious teen comedy.

on 14+

★★★★★

Director: Mark Waters **Cast:** Lindsay Lohan, Rachel McAdams, Tina Fey **Running time:** 97 minutes **Theatrical release date:** 4/30/2004 **Genre:** Comedy **MPAA rating:** PG-13

Looking for a smart teen comedy for your older kids? Try this edgy movie, which features some mature material but also some surprising insights into the high school social scene. Be aware that the movie includes some pretty racy stuff, including crude humor (a dog bites a woman's false breasts), sexual references, underage drinking, and strong profanity. The girls are cruel to each other, although they eventually learn that such behavior isn't acceptable. The themes will ring true to high school kids, and the movie might inspire them to open up about their own experiences dealing with cliques, popularity, and competition.

DVD note: *On the Special Collector's Edition, expect some sexually charged slang and topics in the featurettes ("nipple sensitivity," "slut"), deleted scenes (references to virginity and pregnancy), and blooper reel ("rubbers").*

Miracle on 34th Street

Classic holiday movie for the whole family.

on 6+

★★★★☆

Director: George Seaton **Cast:** Natalie Wood, Maureen O'Hara, Edmund Gwenn **Running time:** 96 minutes **Theatrical release date:** 5/2/1947 **Genre:** Classics **MPAA rating:** NR

This sweet holiday tale (the original version starring Natalie Wood, Maureen O'Hara, and Edmund Gwenn) will charm kids and kids at heart. The simple story of a little girl who comes to believe in Santa Claus is as heartwarming as you remember from your own childhood. Kids will be immediately drawn to Kris Kringle and young Susan. Content-wise, there's little to worry about; the Macy's branding throughout is about as iffy as it gets. The focus here is more on Santa, as opposed to the religious aspects of Christmas, but there are also lessons about the importance of childhood wonder, trust, imagination, and standing up for what you believe. Even cynical kids will find themselves wanting to believe in Santa again. The 1994 remake is sweet, too, if not a true classic.

Modern Times

Families will cherish Chaplin's silent slapstick.

on 6+

★★★★★

Director: Charlie Chaplin **Cast:** Charlie Chaplin, Paulette Godard, Stanley Sandford **Running time:** 87 minutes **Theatrical release date:** 2/5/1936 **Genre:** Classics **MPAA rating:** NR

The film is Chaplin's in more ways than one—not only does he star in it, but he also wrote, produced, and directed it and composed the music. His character is simply "a worker," tightening bolts on a factory assembly line, overseen by an overbearing boss. The comedy of errors that ensues lands the "worker" in and out of jail; he breaks out, attempts to get thrown in, and ultimately finds love. Chaplin's signature style and genius physical comedy transcend the film's lack of spoken dialogue (talkies had hit the silver screen by 1936, but Chaplin opted to go silent). Expect plenty of smoking; it was standard practice for the '30s. Today's kids, used to special effects and digital blockbusters, might be reluctant to watch this classic at first. But Chaplin's work is a great introduction to film history for young movie buffs, and it won't be lost on fans of modern-day comic actors like Jim Carrey and Robin Williams.

Monsters, Inc.

Cuddly, adorable, kid-friendly monster movie.

Director: Pete Docter, David Silverman, Lee Unkrich
Cast: John Goodman, Billy Crystal, Mary Gibbs **Running time:** 92 minutes
Theatrical release date: 11/2/2001 **Genre:** Animated **MPAA rating:** G

Wouldn't think of taking your five-year-old to a monster movie? Don't worry about this one, because it's cuddly and adorable. Here, the monsters (who pass through closets from their world into ours) are just doing their job–any kid can see that. They work in the scare factory nine-to-five, where kids' screams are turned into energy. No scared kids, no electricity. But one little girl who enters their world by mistake isn't scared–she makes friends with monster Sulley, who hides her from the alarmist authorities. Everyone is actually scared of *her*, except creepy Randall, who captures her and tries to take her screams by force. That scene, a terrific high-wire-act chase, and a scene in which monsters in hazmat suits shave another monster (he touched a kid's sock!), make this a little too scary for preschoolers, but perfect for anyone ready to face the dreaded closet monster.

Monty Python and the Holy Grail

Nonstop hilarity for families; some bawdy humor.

Director: Terry Gilliam, Terry Jones **Cast:** Graham Chapman, John Cleese, Eric Idle
Running time: 91 minutes **Theatrical release date:** 5/10/1975 **Genre:** Comedy
MPAA rating: PG

Utter silliness never gets old. The British comedy troupe that made a name for itself in the '70s has caused generations to double over in painful laughter while watching this unbelievably absurd take on the King Arthur legend. Arthur's knights encounter French tauntings; shrubbery-obsessed foes who say "Ni!"; a castle full of vestal virgins (who ask to be spanked and request oral sex–the one scene that warrants keeping the remote handy for a quick pause or fast-forward . . .); a murderous rabbit; a limbless, blood-spurting knight who still wants to fight ("it's only a flesh wound"); and God, animated, sarcastic, and annoyed at humans (the Pythons don't think God is out of bounds, so be prepared, especially if kids ask to see *The Life of Brian* next). If it wasn't for the bawdiness, all kids could enjoy. But don't let teens miss out on this bit of comic genius.

Moulin Rouge

Dazzling musical romance for teens.

on 15+

★★★★

Director: Baz Luhrmann **Cast:** Nicole Kidman, Ewan McGregor, John Leguizamo **Running time:** 127 minutes **Theatrical release date:** 6/1/2001 **Genre:** Musical **MPAA rating:** PG-13

This spectacular musical masterpiece has director Baz Luhrman's trademark flair. There's a heartwarming simplicity to the story, which argues that the most important things in life are freedom, beauty, truth, and (above all) love. Set in 1899, the movie follows hopeless romantic poet Christian (Ewan McGregor) as he arrives in Paris to join the Bohemian revolution. He meets Satine (Nicole Kidman), a star at the Moulin Rouge cabaret who has visions of grandeur. Their forbidden love story meets with chaos and treachery from those around them, but their love is unbroken. The tunes are passionate (McGregor and Kidman sing) and modern (Nirvana, Madonna, and more), serving as literal interpretations of the story. Expect drinking, sexual references and situations (Satine is a courtesan), and a generally decadent atmosphere. Characters are driven by wealth, money, and power–but Christian reminds everyone, quite literally, that all you need is love.

DVD note: *On the two-disc Collector's Edition, several featurettes and interviews discuss sexuality, debauchery, fetishes, and prostitution. Both the live performance of and music video for "Lady Marmalade" feature sexually explicit costumes and choreography.*

Mrs. Doubtfire

You'll laugh, you'll cry. Best divorce movie.

on 12+ ★★★★

Director: Chris Columbus **Cast:** Robin Williams, Sally Field, Pierce Brosnan **Running time:** 125 minutes **Theatrical release date:** 11/24/1993 **Genre:** Comedy **MPAA rating:** PG-13

Robin Williams stars as actor Daniel Hillard, who becomes Mary Poppins-like nanny Mrs. Doubtfire to his own children after divorce deprives him of unsupervised visitation rights. As funny as this movie is, it's really about the pain of separation and divorce. Serious issues–like the perception that Daniel is a bad father because he doesn't make a lot of money and the implied criticism of careerist mother Miranda (Sally Field)–are buried under a lot of padding and jokes. Kids whose families are going through divorce might find this movie both reassuring and painful in spots (particularly the separations as seen from the parental perspective). Those who fear separation might want to wait to see this until they feel more safe and secure, but some may find the movie helpful because it lessens feelings of being alone or unique.

DVD note: *On the Standard Edition, cast interviews mention homosexuality, makeup test footage includes the word "s--t," and the deleted scenes are full of strong language ("f--king bitch" being the worst), and mention alcohol and spousal abuse.*

Mulan

Disneyfied but dignified tale of Chinese warrior.

Director: Tony Bancroft, Barry Cook **Cast:** Ming-Na, Eddie Murphy, Harvey Fierstein **Running time:** 88 minutes **Theatrical release date:** 6/19/1998 **Genre:** Animated **MPAA rating:** G

It takes a brave, determined girl to defy her father in order to save him. Mulan, who was supposed to be "training" to be a proper Chinese bride, pretends to be a boy and takes her injured father's place in secret when he's called up to fight the Huns. She trains and fights with men, is found out and made an outcast, and still manages to save China and bring her family honor. This is a movie guaranteed to choke up dads and daughters everywhere. And though it's a decidedly Disneyfied take on a Chinese fairy tale (no memorable tunes, but Eddie Murphy plays the bumbling dragon sidekick), elements of

Chinese culture and history ring true. With some scary battle scenes and gender stereotypes culled for laughs, it's a good dad-daughter movie night for ages five and up.

The Muppet Movie

Classic first big-screen outing for Jim Henson's Muppets.

Director: James Frawley **Cast:** Jim Henson, Frank Oz, Jerry Nelson **Running time:** 95 minutes **Theatrical release date:** 6/22/1979 **Genre:** Comedy **MPAA rating:** G

It may not be easy being green, but it's a walk in the park for Kermit the Frog and his Muppet pals to entertain kids. Their first big-screen outing–in which Kermit, Fozzie Bear, Miss Piggy, and pals head to Hollywood to seek their fortune, dodging frog leg-obsessed bad guy Doc Hopper (Charles Durning) along the way–is still the best (other standouts include *The Great Muppet Caper*, *The Muppets Take Manhattan*, and *The Muppet Christmas Carol*). The familiar Muppet characters and broad gags are sure to entertain younger viewers, while grown-ups will enjoy the parade of cameos by big-name actors (a Muppet tradition) and some of the more deadpan humor. Even better, there are some nice messages about friendship and persistence for kids to take away.

The Music Man

Glorious production, with gorgeous music, dancing.

on 6+
★★★★★

Director: Morton DaCosta **Cast:** Robert Preston, Buddy Hackett, Shirley Jones **Running time:** 151 minutes **Theatrical release date:** 6/19/1962 **Genre:** Musical **MPAA rating:** G

If they were going to remake this classic musical right, they'd have to put rapper Jay-Z or Kanye West in the lead. Robert Preston drops some dope rhymes ("Ya got trouble, right here in River City") as the fast-talking con man posing as a bandleader. "Sadder but wiser" Marion has met his type before (just ask the gossipy town ladies, though it's all vague speculation), but she still falls for him–and who wouldn't? The stubborn Iowa townsfolk add a whole lot of fun, with a barbershop quartet and giddy songs like "Pick-a-Little

Talk-a-Little" and "Shipoopi." By the time the seventy-six trombones arrive on the Wells Fargo wagon, kids will be itching to join a band and visit River City all over again.

My Big Fat Greek Wedding

The perfect sleepover movie for tween girls (and their moms, too!)

Director: Joel Zwick **Cast:** Nia Vardalos, Michael Constantine, John Corbett
Running time: 95 minutes **Theatrical release date:** 8/2/2002 **Genre:** Comedy
MPAA rating: PG

The story behind this movie is as remarkable as the film itself. Actress/writer Nia Vardalos created a one-woman show about her Greek family and their response when she married a man who wasn't Greek. Tom Hanks and his wife, Rita Wilson (who *is* Greek), saw the show and decided to make it into a movie with Vardalos playing herself. You and your kids will fall in love with Vardalos and her family, too, as they try to come to grips with the fact that their spinster daughter has found love with a non-Greek. The movie offers a great way to talk about people who come from different ethnic, racial, or religious backgrounds. Do your kids know any families like that? What kind of challenges did they face? What kind of new traditions came from blending the differences? And if you don't feel like talking about anything, just sit back and enjoy this great (and age-appropriate) romance.

My Fair Lady

Tuneful, witty, stylish musical to entertain all ages.

Director: George Cukor **Cast:** Audrey Hepburn, Rex Harrison, Stanley Holloway **Running time:** 170 minutes **Theatrical release date:** 12/25/1964 **Genre:** Musical **MPAA rating:** G

"With a little bit o' luck," kids will discover this witty, wonderful musical about street peddler Eliza Doolittle (Audrey Hepburn), who becomes a fair lady with the help of uppity linguist Henry Higgins (Rex Harrison). Worth seeing for the charismatic lead performances alone, kids will also get roped in by the festive songs ("On the plain! In Spain!" "I'm getting married in the morning") and the lush costumes and sets (what hats!). The "bring me my slippers" relationship between Eliza and Henry can get grating (especially with a reference he makes to a possible beating for misbehaving), but ultimately sexism is shown as a handicap. Drinking is shown that way, too, when viewers meet Eliza's deadbeat dad, but it's also played for laughs. This rather long classic makes for a "loverly" couple nights of viewing for ages six and up.

My Neighbor Totoro

on 5+
★★★★★

One of the best family movies of all time.

Director: Hayao Miyazaki **Cast:** Cheryl Chase, Dakota Fanning, Frank Welker **Running time:** 86 minutes **Theatrical release date:** 10/23/2005 **Genre:** Animated **MPAA rating:** G

Japanese Animator Hayao Mizayaki is best known for *Spirited Away* (2003) and *Howl's Moving Castle* (2005). But this is the movie that gave this master filmmaker his U.S. start. It tells the story of two sisters, ten-year-old Satsuki and four-year-old Mei, who move to the country with their father to be closer to their mother, who's recovering in a nearby hospital from an unnamed illness. While exploring the forest near their house, the two girls discover creatures–which, according to the wise old woman next door, only the young can see. There are soot sprites; furry, protective, bunny-like Totoros; and a magic bus in the shape of a cat. The girls are enchanted by these mystical creatures and the magical forest they inhabit. There aren't any villains, scary monsters, or cranky adults. Instead, Miyazaki presents a father who is both physically and mentally present in the lives of his children and sisters who act like real siblings. Satsuki and Mei fight, make mischief, and more often than not get along. Without syrupy sweet sentimentality, viewers are privy to a family that genuinely loves one another. Prepare to watch this one over and over.

Napoleon Dynamite

One-of-a-kind high school comedy for the family.

Director: Jared Hess **Cast:** Jon Heder, Jon Gries, Efren Ramirez
Running time: 82 minutes **Theatrical release date:** 8/27/2004 **Genre:** Comedy
MPAA rating: PG

Far from your typical high school comedy, the movie captures a character that kids will laugh at, ponder, relate to, and above all, imitate. Napoleon, best friend Pedro, and love interest Deb forge a friendship through their misfit status. Older oddball brother Kip and Uncle Rico (who still relishes in the days of high-school heroism) round out a cast of characters trying to find love, success, and friendship–all in their own hilariously immature and misguided way. Heder's unique take on Napoleon quickly ushered the film into cult status with his quirky antics and comedic timing. Accidents are used for physical comedy and other than Rico trying to sell herbal breast enhancements to high school girls, there's hardly anything offensive. Parents should be prepared for kids to talk like Napoleon, whose signature phrases, "idiot," "sweet," and "gosh," will become staples in your home.

DVD note: *On the Standard Edition, one deleted scene and the short film "Peluca" show some pushing and fighting, plus students are shown illegally buying lottery tickets.*

The NeverEnding Story

A book-loving boy gets caught up in his own fantasy tale.

Director: Wolfgang Petersen **Cast:** Noah Hathaway, Alan Oppenheimer, Patricia Hayes
Running time: 102 minutes **Theatrical release date:** 7/20/1984 **Genre:** Fantasy
MPAA rating: PG

Based on the German novel by Michael Ende, this tween-friendly film tells the story of young Bastian, who discovers *The NeverEnding Story* in an old bookstore. He quickly becomes engrossed in the fantasy as he reads about boy warrior Atreyu, who's trying to save the land of Fantasia. In the end, a child's imagination is needed to save the empire from destruction, which ultimately calls for Bastian to become a character within the story he's reading. While the overall message encourages kids to become book lovers, the adventures that take place within the film might scare very young children. Potentially upsetting incidents involve a bloody battle, a steamrolling rock-monster, and a beloved horse being sucked into a swamp. But the message of daring to dream and soaring to new heights through books is a powerful one.

A Night at the Opera

Marx Brothers masterpiece is still hilarious.

on 8+
★★★★★

Director: Sam Wood **Cast:** Groucho Marx, Chico Marx, Harpo Marx
Running time: 96 minutes **Theatrical release date:** 11/15/1935 **Genre:** Classics
MPAA rating: UR

Looking for a laugh-out-loud comedy the whole family can enjoy? Check out this comedy classic starring the Marx Brothers. Although kids may initially turn their noses up at something so "old," those who give it a chance will be paid back in belly laughs. The silly slapstick will appeal to younger kids, while the clever wordplay will amuse tweens, teens, and parents. Unlike most modern comedies, there's no potty humor or offensive language to worry about; pratfalls are as violent as things get, as this is "Three Stooges Lite." Although the Marx Brothers play characters who aren't very nice–they steal, cheat, lie, and cause havoc–it's unlikely that kids are going to focus on the moral behaviors. They'll be too busy laughing! Afterward, check out other Marx Brothers classics like *A Day at the Races*, *Horse Feathers*, and *Duck Soup*.

The Nightmare before Christmas

Tim Burton magic with just a touch of scariness.

Director: Tim Burton **Cast:** Chris Sarandon, Catherine O'Hara, Paul Reubens **Running time:** 76 minutes **Theatrical release date:** 10/29/1993 **Genre:** Animated **MPAA rating:** PG

This movie is a magical stop-motion animation marvel. Offbeat director Burton has fashioned a funny, darkish tale that pokes a bit of fun at kids' two favorite holidays (indeed, only the Easter Bunny is spared). The story revolves around Jack Skellington (voiced by Chris Sarandon), the Pumpkin King—a creature who is to Halloween what Santa is to Christmas. When Jack becomes bored with staging yet another fright night for the sketchy members of Halloweentown, he wanders away and stumbles across Christmastown—and becomes immediately entranced. This being a Halloween movie, there are some scary creatures and skeletons (particularly villain Oogie Boogie). And some kids may be a bit confused about how Christmas is affected. But this pleasant respite from some of the more saccharine holiday movies is so inventive that it's great fun for whole-family viewing.

North by Northwest

Witty thriller from the master of suspense Alfred Hitchcock.

Director: Alfred Hitchcock **Cast:** Cary Grant, Eva Marie Saint, James Mason **Running time:** 136 minutes **Theatrical release date:** 7/28/1959 **Genre:** Action/ Adventure **MPAA rating:** NR

The image of Cary Grant running from a low-flying crop duster may be one of the most iconic images from one of cinema's most legendary directors. *North by Northwest* is the perfect "starter Hitchcock" film for older tweens who like good suspense stories. Grant stars as Roger Thornhill, an advertising executive who gets mistaken for a spy named George Kaplan. Before he knows what's happening, he's drawn into a web of intrigue (accompanied by classic Hitchcock blonde Eva Marie Saint) that eventually leads to a thrilling sequence atop Mt. Rushmore. Expect a few double entendres and some drinking and smoking (it was made in the '50s, after all), but the nonstop tension is the big issue here–some kids just aren't ready for that. Those who are might also enjoy other Hitchcock classics like *Rear Window* and *Vertigo*, but save *Psycho* for older teens.

Of Mice and Men

An elegant adaptation of Steinbeck's classic Depression-era novel.

Director: Gary Sinise **Cast:** John Malkovich, Gary Sinise, Ray Walston **Running time:** 115 minutes **Theatrical release date:** 10/2/1992 **Genre:** Drama **MPAA rating:** PG-13

This modest, sincere adaptation of John Steinbeck's Depression-era classic is a must-see for teens reading the book in English class–and kids who haven't read it may be inspired to pick up a copy after watching. The onscreen chemistry between Gary Sinise and John Malkovich and the faithful-to-the-novel script combine to make this a gripping, emotionally intense drama. There's some violence, including fistfights, a man shooting his dog, an accidental killing, and a main character's very upsetting death. There's some minor swearing and the use of a racial slur. It's definitely not the feel-good movie of the year, but mature kids can handle the heavy themes. The shocking ending is sure to inspire a lot of conversation about whether or not George did the right thing.

Old Yeller

Tearjerker is one of the best early Disney dramas.

Director: Robert Stevenson **Cast:** Dorothy McGuire, Fess Parker, Jeff York **Running time:** 83 minutes **Theatrical release date:** 12/25/1957 **Genre:** Drama **MPAA rating:** G

Kids who love animals will be touched by Disney's classic drama about a boy and his beloved dog. Based on Fred Gipson's novel, the film focuses on young Travis and the profound effect a yellow stray has on his life. But it's definitely a tearjerker, so have tissues handy! There are some scary confrontations between Old Yeller and a bear, wild boars, and a wolf. Travis' father leaves the family to go on a cattle drive; kids may be alarmed by his temporary absence. Parents looking for a good movie about loss won't need to look further–this one handles Old Yeller's death in a sensitive and age-appropriate way.

Oliver!

Glorious musical based on *Oliver Twist*.

Director: Carol Reed **Cast:** Mark Lester, Ron Moody, Oliver Reed
Running time: 153 minutes **Theatrical release date:** 12/10/1968 **Genre:** Musical
MPAA rating: G

Harry Potter and his cupboard under the stairs have nothing on Oliver, Charles Dickens' orphan who gets expelled from his dour orphanage onto the streets, where he has to "pick a pocket or two" just to survive. Oliver meets both sticky-fingered friends and murderous enemies before he finds a permanent home in this lavish, classic musical rife with memorable songs ("Consider Yourself," "Who Will Buy"). Some scenes are too jarring for younger kids–especially the off-screen killing of a main character by her husband–and there's a lot of drinking in bars, but there's also plenty to enjoy with tweens and plenty of discussion to be had about class issues and Dickens' unforgettable characters, their motivations, and their moral choices.

The Pagemaster

An entertaining film little kids will enjoy, full of positive messages.

Director: Pixote Hunt, Maurice Hunt, Joe Johnston **Cast:** Macaulay Culkin, Christopher Lloyd, Ed Begley Jr. **Running time:** 80 minutes Release date: 11/23/1994
Genre: Fantasy **MPAA rating:** G

While seeking refuge from a wild storm, cowardly Richard Tyler (Macaulay Culkin) stumbles upon an eerie library. After slipping on a wet floor and being knocked unconscious, he's sent on a magical journey in a cartoon fantasy world controlled by the Pagemaster (Christopher Lloyd). Befriended by the personified books Adventure, Fantasy, and Horror, Rich leads the gang through the mysterious and unpredictable world of the Pagemaster, facing his fears as he tackles threatening characters like Moby Dick, Mr. Hyde, Long John Silver, and a fire-breathing dragon (but nothing is too scary). This charming movie is imaginative and full of good messages. It unleashes the power of books and highlights the importance of facing your fears. Not only will it make younger kids laugh, but–more importantly–it will make them learn.

The Parent Trap

Hayley Mills rocks in her dual role as twins.

ON 6+

★★★★

Director: David Swift **Cast:** Hayley Mills, Maureen O'Hara, Brian Keith **Running time:** 129 minutes **Theatrical release date:** 6/21/61 **Genre:** Comedy **MPAA rating:** G

This wholesome family comedy, though a bit dated, still manages to engage both kids and adults. Although the younger set may be more interested in the 1998 remake because it stars Lindsay Lohan, the original Haley Mills version still has lots of charm. The premise is simple: Long-separated twins meet at summer camp and decide to change places, hoping to bring their divorced parents back together. Content-wise, some dated gender stereotyping is as bad as it gets. Some kids may be alarmed at the idea of the twins being split up, and divorced parents may need to remind kids that most couples don't reunite. The twins are mischievous, but their intentions are good. Check out the remake as well, and ask kids which they prefer and why.

Pee-wee's Big Adventure

Just as charming and curious as it was in 1985.

ON 6+

★★★★

Director: Tim Burton **Cast:** Paul Reubens, Elizabeth Daily, Mark Holton **Running time:** 90 minutes **Theatrical release date:** 8/9/1985 **Genre:** Comedy **MPAA rating:** PG

This isn't your typical Tim Burton movie. It's a totally goofy road trip comedy about a boy and his stolen bike–only that "boy" is a tall, skinny man named Pee-wee. Pee-wee's mission takes him to a biker bar (his "Tequila" dance in platform shoes is priceless), a dinosaur-museum truck stop, the Alamo (where there *is* no basement–who knew?), and eventually Hollywood. Kids will love Pee-wee's giddy laugh and his innocent outlook (he'd rather be with his bike than get romantic with his friend Dottie at the drive-in), but younger kids may be scared by the ghostly Large Marge and some other sinister dream images of clowns and devils. (Beware: A rock video pops up briefly of Twisted Sister shouting "Burn in Hell.") Parents with a taste for the offbeat will love this road trip back to the '80s, too.

Pirates of the Caribbean: The Curse of the Black Pearl

Rip-roaring fun for kids who don't mind skeletons.

Director: Gore Verbinski **Cast:** Johnny Depp, Orlando Bloom, Keira Knightley **Running time:** 143 minutes **Theatrical release date:** 7/9/2003 **Genre:** Action/Adventure **MPAA rating:** PG-13

Avast, matey! Have ye met Captain Jack Sparrow? Odds are ye have, since Johnny Depp's dapper Captain Jack and his band of merry miscreants have quickly become some of the movies' most memorable characters. Their first cinematic voyage is by far the best of the bunch (*Dead Man's Chest* and *At World's End* get increasingly convoluted), especially considering it was based on a Disney theme-park ride. Expect a bit of ribaldry (oh, those tight corsets!), plenty of rum drinking, some colorful pirate language, and lots and lots and *lots* of skeletons. Older tweens who don't mind the graphically ghostly crew–or gags like a fake eyeball repeatedly popping out of a pirate's face (and getting speared by a fork at one point)–will be wildly entertained by this swashbuckling adventure, but sensitive kids might need to take it slow . . . and watch with the lights on.

DVD note: *On the two-disc Collector's Edition, you'll find some sexual content (a deleted scene has a woman almost showing nipples, a blooper reel shows Keira Knightly saying, "Might I have something to wear, or will it be bare breasts and ankles all the way?"), plus added violence–some from deleted scenes, and some from the "Below Deck" featurette where an expert describes dismemberment, stabbings, hangings, and other acts of violence and torture.*

Pride and Prejudice

Gorgeous Jane Austen adaptation.

on 10+

★★★★☆

Director: Joe Wright **Cast:** Keira Knightley, Matthew MacFadyen, Donald Sutherland **Running time:** 127 minutes **Theatrical release date:** 12/23/2005 **Genre:** Drama **MPAA rating:** PG

Mix the timeless appeal of Jane Austen with the star power of Keira Knightley, and you have this perfect–and perfectly accessible–adaptation for tweens and teens. Knightley plays Elizabeth Bennet, the second of five daughters in a family whose fortunes are passing to a doltish male cousin, so their mother is in a desperate hurry to marry them off. Elizabeth wants none of it–and she especially isn't about to fall for the proud and pompous Mr. Darcy. (Doth the lady protest too much?) It's hard not to get caught up in this rocky yet innocent romance, the complex social mores of the day, the balls (where there's some drinking), the gossip, the proposals, and the splendor–beautiful dresses, estates, and countryside. Once you get sucked into Austen's world, there are plenty more adaptations to try–like 1995's excellent *Sense and Sensibility*.

The Princess Bride

Witty, winsome fairy tale for the whole family.

on 8+

★★★★★

Director: Rob Reiner **Cast:** Cary Elwes, Mandy Patinkin, Robin Wright Penn **Running time:** 98 minutes **Theatrical release date:** 9/25/1987 **Genre:** Comedy **MPAA rating:** PG

One of the best fairy tales without "Brothers Grimm" or "Hans Christian Andersen" in its pedigree, Rob Reiner's charmingly cracked comedy can be enjoyed at many different levels. Tweens will love the romance, swashbuckling sword fights, and derring-do (not to mention Fezzik's penchant for silly rhymes), while older teens and parents will appreciate the wry humor and pointed references (the one to a certain land war in Asia comes to mind . . .). Inigo's revenge fixation is fairly intense (at one point, his failure sends him on a drinking binge), the Fire Swamp scenes may frighten some younger kids–the R.O.U.S. attack is particularly alarming–and Westley's torture and apparent demise are upsetting. But the lighthearted script and delightful performances carry the day in the end. Just watch out for those shrieking eels...

The Princess Diaries

Terrific fun for girls and their families, too.

on 6+

★★★★★

Director: Garry Marshall **Cast:** Anne Hathaway, Julie Andrews, Hector Elizondo **Running time:** 115 minutes **Theatrical release date:** 8/3/2001 **Genre:** Comedy **MPAA rating:** G

"Just in case I'm not enough of a freak already, let's add a tiara!" Mia Thermopolis shouts when she finds out she's a real princess, not just another awkward teen. Based on Meg Cabot's bestseller, this is the ultimate makeover movie for moms and daughters to enjoy together. Moms will love Julie Andrews' turn as the Queen of Genovia (or "Grandma," as Mia calls her), and they'll love seeing mom and daughter bond over rock-climbing walls, painting sessions, and conversations about whether Mia should accept her crown. Kids will love Mia's cool car, her bossy friend Lilly, and the romantic tension as Mia falls in love and gets her first kiss. Mia drives without a license (escaping a ticket with Grandma in a sneaky fashion) and mourns her dead father, but there's nothing else to keep whole families from enjoying this modern fairy tale.

Raiders of the Lost Ark

A thrill ride and a half.

on 12+

★★★★★

Director: Steven Spielberg **Cast:** Harrison Ford, Karen Allen, Paul Freeman **Running time:** 115 minutes **Theatrical release date:** 6/12/1981 **Genre:** Action/Adventure **MPAA rating:** PG

"Snakes. I hate snakes." But Indiana Jones loves his fedora, his whip, dangerous ancient artifacts, and doing anything and everything to get his hands on them—even wading through a pit of asps. Action-loving kids will be in heaven; fists and swords fly on moving trucks, planes, horses, trains, and cargo ships. But some grisly and frightening scenes (a man's head meets a propeller, ghosts attack, faces melt) make this an actioner for stronger stomachs. Add to that some heavy drinking by Indiana's tough heroine and the omnipresent signs of the Third Reich, and parents will want to save this Steven Spielberg blockbuster for movie night with older tweens and teens.

Real Women Have Curves

Ugly Betty star captivates in teen drama.

on 14+

★★★★★

Director: Patricia Cardoso **Cast:** America Ferrera, Lupe Ontiveros, Ingrid Oliu **Running time:** 90 minutes **Theatrical release date:** 11/8/2002 **Genre:** Drama **MPAA rating:** PG-13

Here's a smart teen drama that's perfect for teens who are sick of movies featuring pampered Caucasian kids–this isn't *Laguna Beach*, and that's a good thing. The fact that it stars America Ferrera, star of *Ugly Betty* and *The Sisterhood of the Traveling Pants*, is another reason older kids will be interested. The story centers on heroine Ana's struggle to be true to herself while respecting her working-class Mexican American family's conservative values. She loses her virginity (nothing much is shown), sneaks out to meet her boyfriend, and enlists her grandfather in a lie. There's also some profanity. But mostly, Ana's a great model for any teen learning to love herself as she grows into an adult, and overall, this is a refreshing movie that could lead to a discussion about culture, body image, and growing up.

DVD note: *On the Standard Edition, the featurettes contain some salty language in Spanish, including "cojones" (balls), "puta" (whore), and "chichis" (tits).*

Remember the Titans

Inspiring football drama brings history to life.

on 8+

★★★★

Director: Boaz Yakin **Cast:** Denzel Washington, Will Patton, Wood Harris **Running time:** 113 minutes **Theatrical release date:** 9/29/2000 **Genre:** Drama **MPAA rating:** PG

This inspiring sports film is based on the real-life 1971 integration of the football team at T.C. Williams High School in Alexandria, Virginia–a bold act that created the only mixed-race team in a football-loving district. In time (of course), the team achieves a sense of brotherhood and camaraderie that transcends race. Families will enjoy watching the raw recruits learning honor and loyalty on the field and translating it into their everyday lives. While there are some clichéd moments–like the team bonding in the locker room as they sing Motown tunes–they'll feel fresh to younger kids. Racist comments and situations, locker room insults, and off-screen death are touched on, and the larger issue of civil rights is dominant. While a parent's perspective will be necessary for inquiring minds, this movie really has something for everyone–football fan or not.

The Return of the Pink Panther

Hilarious Inspector Clouseau better in this sequel than the original.

Director: Blake Edwards **Cast:** Peter Sellers, Christopher Plummer, Herbert Lum **Running time:** 113 minutes **Theatrical release date:** 5/21/1975 **Genre:** Comedy **MPAA rating:** G

The original *Pink Panther* is great–don't get us wrong. But kids won't get as full a dose of the hilarious Peter Sellers in that movie as they will here, since David Niven was the real star of the first installment in this side-splitting series. That said, once your kids see this one, they'll want to see the rest, too. The slapstick can't be beat, and the klutzy Clouseau will make you weep with laughter. There are a few suggestive moments that will be completely uninteresting to kids, and Clouseau refers to his Asian manservant, Cato, as his "yellow friend," but to take anything seriously in this movie is to miss out on one of the greatest broad comedies of all time.

Roman Holiday

A delightful classic in romantic Rome.

on 8+
★★★★★

Director: William Wyler **Cast:** Gregory Peck, Audrey Hepburn, Eddie Albert **Running time:** 118 minutes **Theatrical release date:** 8/27/1953 **Genre:** Classics **MPAA rating:** NR

Kids, meet Audrey Hepburn. Girls (and their moms) will love that this utterly captivating actress plays a princess and that she falls in love with a dashing reporter (Gregory Peck as Joe Bradley) when she runs away for a day to escape the pressures of public life. All tweens will be able to follow the plot: Two reporters, knowing who she is and hoping for the scoop of the year, play Rome tour guides for the wide-eyed princess. But when they get to know her, will they really write their tabloid-esque story? The princess' adventures begin after she's given a sleeping pill and ends up (innocently) staying with Joe. From there she sips champagne, tries her first cigarette (and doesn't like it), and ends up falling in the river after a scuffle on a barge—proving that Hepburn is charming even when she's soaking wet.

Rudy

Inspiring sports film about a real life underdog.

Director: David Anspaugh **Cast:** Sean Astin, Jon Favreau, Ned Beatty **Running time:** 116 minutes **Theatrical release date:** 10/13/1993 **Genre:** Drama **MPAA rating:** PG

Are your kids suckers for a good sports movie? Here's an inspiring choice about a real-life underdog who worked hard to beat the odds. Kids will root for Rudy (Sean Astin) as he encounters endless obstacles on his path to playing football for Notre Dame. Rudy isn't particularly gifted or brainy, but through sheer will and with the help of friends, he works toward his lofty goal. There's some mild profanity, football-field brutality, and scenes of emotional intensity as Rudy suffers bitter disappointments. But overall, the drama proves that hard work and perseverance really do pay off. More than the wildest science fiction or fantasy story, *Rudy* will make you believe that anything is possible.

The Sandlot

on 8+

★★★★☆

Field of Dreams for tweens.

Director: David M. Evans **Cast:** Tom Guiry, Mike Vitar, Patrick Renna
Running time: 101 minutes **Theatrical release date:** 4/7/1993 **Genre:** Comedy
MPAA rating: PG

Tweens—particularly tween boys—*love* this lighthearted baseball movie. Set during a summer in the early '60s, it follows a group of ragtag kids who live for America's pastime. New kid Scotty (Tom Guiry) doesn't really know a curve ball from a slider when he moves to the neighborhood, but thanks to help from fellow team member Rodriguez (Mike Vitar), he's soon playing like a pro. The main threat to the gang's happiness is the Beast—a giant, slavering dog on the other side of the sandlot fence (he might briefly scare some younger viewers). Expect some mild language, a bit of girl ogling (one boy tricks a lifeguard into kissing him), and some typical "boys will be boys" scuffles. But overall, the movie has a sun-kissed, nostalgic tone that both kids and parents will appreciate.

School of Rock

Standout Jack Black in hilarious nerd-becomes-cool comedy.

Director: Richard Linklater **Cast:** Jack Black, Adam Pascal, Lucas Papaelias
Running time: 108 minutes **Theatrical release date:** 10/3/2003 **Genre:** Comedy
MPAA rating: PG-13

Jack Black stars as loser Dewey Finn, who lives for rock—but when he's fired from his band and runs out of money, he has to grow up. Pretending to be his roommate, Dewey substitutes as a fifth-grade teacher. And—you guessed it—instead of teaching, he forms the group of would-be nerds into a band. But it's the kids who end up teaching Dewey a thing or two about life and pursuing your dreams. If you don't mind crass humor, some strongish language, and some drug and alcohol references, this movie is a great way to talk to your kids about what's important to them and how to balance academics and the fun stuff in their lives.

DVD note: *On the Special Collector's Edition, the "MTV's Diary of Jack Black" featurette contains a blurred-out shot of a nude Jack Black and a* *brief glimpse of his butt crack. The words "kick-ass," "biotch," "bitch," and "hell" are used (and "f--k" is bleeped out).*

The Secret of NIMH

Fascinating, but sensitive animal-lovers beware.

on 8+

★★★★

Director: Don Bluth **Cast:** Elizabeth Hartman, Derek Jacobi, Arthur Malet **Running time:** 82 minutes **Theatrical release date:** 7/2/1982 **Genre:** Animated **MPAA rating:** G

This movie is based on Robert C. O'Brien's prize-winning book *Mrs. Frisby and the Rats of N.I.M.H.* Mrs. Brisby (the character's last name was changed for the movie) is a widowed mouse living on a farm with her four children, including Timmy, who's bedridden with pneumonia. When they're forced to find a new home, the Great Owl advises Mrs. Brisby to seek the help of Nicodemus, the king of a colony of intelligent rats who escaped from an animal laboratory. It's suspenseful and somewhat dark at times and touches on themes of animal cruelty and experimentation. The worst part for sensitive viewers: A flashback shows the animated animals being experimented on–it's a bit spacey and might require some parental explanation.

Selena

J-Lo hits the right notes in Tejano star's tale.

on 9+

★★★★

Director: Gregory Nava **Cast:** Jennifer Lopez, Jackie Guerra, Constance Marie **Running time:** 127 minutes **Theatrical release date:** 3/21/1997 **Genre:** Drama **MPAA rating:** PG

This touching, effervescent, and ultimately tragic biopic will fascinate tweens and teens, especially those who are fans of star Jennifer Lopez. The movie tells the story of Grammy-winning Tejano singer Selena, who was killed at age twenty-three by her fan club president. Although the film occasionally feels somewhat sugar-coated, it remains a very watchable, entertaining, and moving tribute to a beloved performer. Kids may ask questions about the events surrounding Selena's murder; it's not shown, but one character does hold a gun to her own head. There's also some mild profanity and gender and racial discrimination. The movie offers a great opportunity to talk about fame and family and may inspire families to check out Tejano music.

Shrek

Gross-out laughs meet a marvelous fairy-tale mix.

on 6+ ★★★★★

Director: Andrew Adamson, Vicky Jenson **Cast:** Mike Myers, Eddie Murphy, Cameron Diaz **Running time:** 90 minutes **Theatrical release date:** 5/18/2001 **Genre:** Animated **MPAA rating:** PG

Dying for an animated movie that you'll enjoy as much as your kids do? Look no further–*Shrek* is the perfect mix of broad, kid-friendly gags and edgy, adult-oriented in-jokes (including innuendoes that will likely go right over a child's head). Mike Myers is flawlessly cast as the voice of the titular ogre, who wants nothing more than to be left alone in his swamp. But when vain Lord Farquaad dumps a swarm of wacky fairy-tale creatures on Shrek's doorstep, the grouchy green guy makes a deal, reluctantly teaming up with chatterbox Donkey (Eddie Murphy, perfecting the sidekick patter he used in *Mulan*) to rescue Princess Fiona in Farquaad's stead. Expect some strongish language for a kids' movie ("damn," "crap") and a fair number of gross-out bodily humor jokes. It's all part of the Shrek package, which continues in the entertaining sequels, *Shrek 2* and *Shrek the Third*.

Singin' in the Rain

Often considered the finest musical of all time.

Director: Stanley Donen, Gene Kelly **Cast:** Gene Kelly, Donald O'Connor, Debbie Reynolds **Running time:** 103 minutes **Theatrical release date:** 4/11/1952 **Genre:** Musical **MPAA rating:** NR

When it comes to pure feel-good movie scenes, it's hard to beat watching a lovestruck Gene Kelly gleefully splishing and splashing his way down a rainy street. This delightful musical about the advent of "talkies" in Hollywood is one of the all-time greats, and kids as young as six will enjoy the lighthearted humor, the physical comedy (particularly in Donald O'Connor's showstopping "Make 'Em Laugh" performance), and the sweet romance between Kelly and Debbie Reynolds. If your kids seem interested in the history behind the movie, try some classic Charlie Chaplin and Buster Keaton silent films; *Modern Times* would be a great start.

The Sisterhood of the Traveling Pants

Sensitive portrayal of four girls' friendships.

Director: Ken Kwapis **Cast:** Amber Tamblyn, Alexis Bledel, America Ferrara
Running time: 119 minutes **Theatrical release date:** 6/1/2005 **Genre:** Drama
MPAA rating: PG

This coming-of-age drama based on the popular book series by Ann Brashares will resonate with tween and teen girls. The cast is filled with names that are easily recognizable to older kids, such as Alexis Bledel (*Gilmore Girls*) and America Ferrera (*Ugly Betty*), and the story of four high school friends' summer adventures will appeal to them. That said, there *is* some edgy material here, including a character losing her virginity, a parent's suicide, the disease/death of a close friend, a father's remarriage, and tense family scenes. There's also some mild profanity and drinking. The movie offers a great opening for a discussion about love, loss, and loyalty. Kids who love the book series can discuss whether or not the movie is a good adaptation.

Snow White and the Seven Dwarfs

Still a delight, with memorable songs and characters.

Director: David Hand **Cast:** Adriana Caselotti, Lucille La Verne, Roy Atwell
Running time: 83 minutes **Theatrical release date:** 2/4/1938 **Genre:** Animated
MPAA rating: G

Heigh ho, heigh ho, it's off to watch a classic you and your kids go! Disney's first full-length animated feature is still one of its best, boasting beautiful animation and great songs ("Whistle While You Work," "Heigh Ho," "Someday My Prince Will Come"). Snow White may not be the most girl-powered heroine, and some of the scenes featuring the evil Queen are downright scary—particularly when she first transforms into the crone and, later, when she breathlessly urges Snow White to taste the poisoned apple—but most kids will be familiar enough with fairy-tale rules to know that Snow's safety (and rescue via handsome prince) is assured. Once you're done watching, see who can name all seven dwarfs faster–you or your kids.

Some Like It Hot

One of the wildest farces ever.

Director: Billy Wilder **Cast:** Tony Curtis, Jack Lemmon, Marilyn Monroe
Running time: 120 minutes **Theatrical release date:** 3/29/1959 **Genre:** Comedy
MPAA rating: NR

With perhaps one of the best last lines in movie history, Billy Wilder's hilarious cross-dressing comedy is great classic to introduce tweens to on family movie night. Jack Lemmon and Tony Curtis are in top form as a pair of Chicago musicians who don wigs and dresses when they go on the run after accidentally witnessing a mob murder (there's lots of shooting during that scene and another late in the movie, but it's mostly off-screen, and it seems tame by today's standards). The innuendoes start flying once the guys meet sweet, curvy Sugar (Marilyn Monroe), but some passionate kisses and a few low-cut gowns are as risqué as it gets. Don't be surprised to see Sugar taking nips from her flask when she's feeling blue–though that's the last thing you'll be after laughing your way through this must-see farce. For fun, see if kids can guess which other Hollywood great Curtis is imitating when he's dressed up as "Junior."

DVD note: *On the Special Edition: The featurette "Nostalgic Look Back" includes Tony Curtis recalling his experiences working as a woman (including the difficulties of urinating while in costume) and the time he saw Marilyn Monroe's breasts.*

The Sound of Music

Outstanding family film features glorious music.

Director: Robert Wise **Cast:** Julie Andrews, Christopher Plummer, Richard Hadyn **Running time:** 174 minutes **Theatrical release date:** 3/2/1965 **Genre:** Musical **MPAA rating:** G

Julie Andrews. Christopher Plummer. An adorable singing brood dressed in curtains. Glorious Austrian Alps as a backdrop. Spectacle, romance, and more spectacle. Song after memorable song ("Do-Re-Mi," "My Favorite Things," "Edelweiss," "So Long, Farewell"). If families haven't watched this classic musical together yet, they should "climb every mountain" to get their hands on it (luckily, they play it on TV around Christmastime every year). Kids younger than six may be frightened by the family's narrow escape from the Nazis and uninterested in the ultra-sweet romance that develops between the captain and his children's new governess. Everyone else: Get out the popcorn and warm up your "Do-Re-Mi"s.

Spaceballs

on 11+
★★★★

Goofy parody mocks the *Star Wars* series.

Director: Mel Brooks **Cast:** Bill Pullman, Daphne Zuniga, Rick Moranis **Running time:** 96 minutes **Theatrical release date:** 6/24/1987 **Genre:** Comedy **MPAA rating:** PG

Spaceballs may not be as artful as Mel Brooks' masterpiece, *Young Frankenstein*, but if you're a *Star Wars* fan, and you're in the mood for a "stupid funny" comedy, you can't go wrong with this goofy parody. Bill Pullman steps into the Han Solo role as Lone Starr, a scruffy hero-for-hire who's sent to rescue spoiled Princess Vespa (Daphne Zuniga) after she's kidnapped by nerdy villain Dark Helmet (Rick Moranis). With the help of his sidekick Barf (John Candy) and an extra boost from the "Schwartz," Lone Starr successfully navigates a barrage of crotch gags and bad puns ("What's the matter, Col. Sanders? Chicken?") to save the day. Your own inner ten-year-old will giggle right along with your tweens at the silly humor; just be ready for some swearing (the "s" word and more) and ethnic humor. On the plus side, the movie's mockery of excessive commercialism could start an interesting discussion.

Spellbound

Every family should see this m-a-r-v-e-l-o-u-s movie.

Director: Jeffrey Blitz **Running time:** 97 minutes **Theatrical release date:** 4/30/2003 **Genre:** Documentary **MPAA rating:** G

This engrossing documentary about the 1999 National Spelling Bee encompasses so much more than knowing how to rattle off complicated words. As it follows the eight featured competitors–who come from a wide range of backgrounds and have very different personalities–it conveys messages about ambition, dedication, and following your dreams. It also sheds a lot of light on the different ways that families communicate and the expectations they have for their kids. Expect some tense competition scenes and some bitterly disappointing losses; the fact that the movie makes you care so much about these kids makes it very emotional when they can't all succeed. Ultimately, like the long, complicated words the kids have to learn, all of the different parts of this movie add up to an impressive whole.

Spider-Man

A fun movie; may be too intense for younger kids.

Director: Sam Raimi **Cast:** Tobey Maguire, Willem Dafoe, Kirsten Dunst **Running time:** 121 minutes **Theatrical release date:** 5/3/2002 **Genre:** Action/Adventure **MPAA rating:** PG-13

He may be able to shoot webs out of his wrists and sense danger, but Spider-Man (aka Peter Parker) is also one of the comic book world's most relatable characters–which is probably one of the reasons he's so popular with tweens and teens. Dealing with feelings of guilt, responsibility, and unrequited (or is it?) love in between doing battle with the menacing Green Goblin, Spidey is a thoughtful hero. Still, he gets involved in a fair amount of explosive action violence, some of which is very intense for younger kids: people are vaporized, impaled, and shot (off-screen), and others (including children) are put in perilous situations. Peter loses one of the people he cares about most and blames himself, and there's a smattering of iffy language and a passionate, rain-soaked kiss between Spider-Man (Tobey Maguire) and love interest Mary

Jane (Kirsten Dunst). Spidey's adventures con- tinue in *Spider-Man 2* (considered the best of the bunch by many fans) and *Spider-Man 3*.

DVD note: *On the Widescreen Special Edition, the "HBO Making of Spider-Man" featurette briefly mentions child abuse. Curse words uttered in the gag/outtake reel and on screen tests are bleeped out. The "Spider-Man: The Mythology of the 21st Century" featurette mentions illegal drugs, death, and the 9/11 terrorist attacks.*

Spirited Away

Magnificent, spellbinding movie with a bit of an edge.

Director: Hayao Miyazaki, Kirk Wise **Cast:** Daveigh Chase, Jason Marsden, Suzanne Pleshette **Running time:** 125 minutes **Theatrical release date:** 9/20/2002 **Genre:** Animated **MPAA rating:** PG

This is a spectacularly beautiful movie–with excellent voice-over work–from the genius who created *My Neighbor Totoro* and *Howl's Moving Castle*. But despite the similar animation style, this isn't a "feel-good" classic like *Totoro*; rather, it's an edgier portrayal of what a young girl needs to do to grow up and take responsibility for more than herself. Chihiro is a sullen ten-year-old who wanders into a world ruled by witches and monsters, where humans are changed into animals. When her parents gorge themselves on enchanted food, they turn into pigs, and Chihiro must overcome her whiny self to enter the spirit world and win them back. The movie has some intense scenes–particularly when Chihiro can't recognize her now porcine parents–that involve separation and a bit of peril. But the movie is blessedly without the saccharine that characterizes so many animated films.

Spy Kids

Just the right combination of fantasy and comedy.

Director: Robert Rodriguez **Cast:** Alexa Vega, Daryl Sabara, Antonio Banderas **Running time:** 88 minutes **Theatrical release date:** 3/30/2001 **Genre:** Action/Adventure **MPAA rating:** PG

Imagine James Bond crossed with *Willy Wonka and the Chocolate Factory*, and you'll have a decent idea of what to expect from this fun, tween-friendly spy flick. After their parents—former agents who "retired" to raise a family—disappear, it's up to Carmen (Alexa Varga) and Juni (Daryl Sabara) Cortez to rescue them . . . and, incidentally, the world. *Spy Kids*' combination of giddy fantasy, exciting adventure, cool gadgets, and sly comedy is sure to make it one of your kids' favorites. Plus, it features strong female and Latino role models. Expect some scenes of peril and (mostly comic) action, as well as some creepy mutant creatures that could scare younger kids. The first sequel, *Spy Kids 2: The Island of Lost Dreams*, is a strong follow up, but *Spy Kids 3-D: Game Over* doesn't measure up.

Stand by Me

Edgy coming-of-age story not for young kids.

on 15+
★★★★

Director: Rob Reiner **Cast:** Wil Wheaton, River Phoenix, Jerry O'Connell **Running time:** 89 minutes **Theatrical release date:** 8/8/1986 **Genre:** Drama **MPAA rating:** R

Between a star-making role for River Phoenix and Rob Reiner's sensitive, skillful script and direction, the movie—which is based on a Stephen King novella—has become a classic. But despite its preteen cast, this isn't a movie for young kids. The story revolves around four small-town twelve-year-old boys who set out on a trek to find a dead body. They overcome oncoming trains, a disgusting bout with leeches, and some threats from a group of older, tougher kids. The movie accurately depicts the painful process of maturation that has plagued tweens and teens for ages. In many ways, the quest's conclusion signifies the end of innocence, since the four boys are never quite the same after making their gruesome discovery. Parents need to know that the language is really rough, some of the content is quite mature, and the kids smoke and drink. This is best reserved for kids going through the rebellious late middle-school/early high-school years—and it's probably a good idea to watch with them. They'll think you're cool for picking the movie, and you'll have a great way to check in with them about some big issues.

DVD note: *On the Special Edition, the interviews in the featurette "Walking the Tracks: The Summer of Stand By Me" use the words "grab-assing" and "Jesus Christ." River Phoenix's untimely death is also discussed in non-graphic terms.*

Star Wars: Episode V: The Empire Strikes Back

They're all great. This is the best of the best.

on 8+

★★★★★

Director: **Irvin Kershner** Cast: **Mark Hamill, Harrison Ford, Carrie Fisher**
Running time: **124 minutes** Theatrical release date: **5/21/1980** Genre: **Action/Adventure** MPAA rating: **PG**

All six *Star Wars* movies are marvelous, but this one is so good that we feel it stands out a bit above the rest. While the 1977 original (*Star Wars: Episode IV: A New Hope*) is also great for eight-year-olds and up, parents, please note: Not all of the movies have the same level of violence. (The more gruesome elements culminate in *Episode III: Revenge of the Sith*, which we recommend for eleven-year-olds and up due to scenes in which children are slaughtered and a key character is charred like a burned-up marshmallow.) And even though you probably already know this, it's worth repeating: *Empire* started out as the middle chapter of the original *Star Wars* trilogy; because of that, it ended with a narrative jolt and an unresolved cliffhanger. Since then, George Lucas has made the three prequels, and viewing them in the new order spoils some of the surprises that shocked 1980 viewers. Aside from plot issues, expect abundant fantasy violence, including lightsaber fights (with limbs cut off), dismemberment, the near-incineration of C-3PO, and the freezing of Han Solo. But you know that everything turns out OK in the end. Just keep to the original three movies for your youngest kids. There will be plenty of time for the more violent movies once they've watched the original three so many times that they know each action sequence by heart.

Superman: The Movie

Super-nostalgic adventure still soars.

Director: Richard Donner **Cast:** Christopher Reeve, Gene Hackman, Margot Kidder **Running time:** 151 minutes **Theatrical release date:** 12/15/1978 **Genre:** Action/Adventure **MPAA rating:** PG

When you're talking superhero sagas, this is how it's done. An unforgettable John Williams anthem ushers our captivating hero from asteroid to adolescence to airborne adulthood. A fascinating villain (Gene Hackman) with a secret lair plots massive destruction with stolen rockets. Superman's nerdy-reporter secret identity introduces him to Lois Lane (Margot Kidder), a lady who may need saving from helicopter crashes, muggers, and earthquakes (she's buried alive in an intense scene) but still has some take-charge '70s-woman flair. While Superman takes a little too long to grow up, and the romantic interludes get pretty cheesy (queue the song "Can You Read My Mind"), this movie that made Christopher Reeve a star will still entrance tweens, teens, and parents flying high on nostalgia.

Swiss Family Robinson

A good introduction for kids reluctant to watch old movies.

Director: Ken Annakin **Cast:** John Mills, Dorothy McGuire, James MacArthur **Running time:** 126 minutes **Theatrical release date:** 12/21/1960 **Genre:** Action/Adventure **MPAA rating:** G

This one's worth watching with your tweens if for no other reason than to show them the Robinsons' fabulous tree house: The multilevel, gadget-packed dwelling is the stuff that dreams are made of when you're eight years old. The good news is that there's lots more to enjoy here as well–the tale of a European family cast away on a seemingly deserted island is a classic adventure (it's based on the book by Johann David Wyss). The characters do battle with some fairly scary pirates and endure other perilous situations–going up against a river snake, a tiger, and more–but they stick together through it all. You'll probably notice some dated stereotyping in the gender roles and the way the pirates are portrayed, but this movie holds up a lot better on that front than some of Disney's other 1960s films.

The Sword in the Stone

Delightful classic brings Arthur legend to life.

Director: Wolfgang Reitherman **Cast:** Rickie Sorensen, Norman Alden, Karl Swenson **Running time:** 79 minutes **Release date:** 12/25/1963 **Genre:** Animated **MPAA rating:** G

Before Arthur pulled the sword from the stone and assembled his knights at a round table, he was a scrappy, scrawny boy nicknamed "Wart" who was bullied by his cousin Kay and given loads of chores by his bristly uncle, Sir Ector. Then he met Merlin, a powerful yet dotty wizard who set out to educate him. Arthur's lessons are whole lot of fun for everyone as he explores the world as a fish, a squirrel, and a bird. Then Merlin teaches him to value "brains over brawn" in a spectacular wizard's duel with the Mad Madam Mim (it can be a little scary for younger viewers). Some catchy tunes round out this often overlooked Disney classic.

This Is Spinal Tap

Hilarious, ribald, drug-filled rock send-up.

on 14+

Director: Rob Reiner **Cast:** Michael McKean, Christopher Guest, Harry Shearer **Running time:** 82 minutes **Theatrical release date:** 3/2/1984 **Genre:** Comedy **MPAA rating:** R

Spinal Tap is a fictional band, and Rob Reiner's classic "mockumentary" about them hilariously highlights their failures. There are moments when the language gets a bit heavy, but they're short and sporadic. Violence and sex are almost nonexistent–except for the songs, which tend to be innuendo-heavy. It *is* a rock movie, so expect lots of references to drugs and alcohol. The movie's humor will likely be lost on kids younger than thirteen or fourteen, and some of the references may even sail over the heads of slightly older kids. But this movie is sure to be a crowd-pleaser for late middle school / early high school boys. They want to push the envelope, and this is a pretty tame way to do it. (If you're a fan of *Best in Show* and *Waiting for Guffman*, don't be surprised if a lot of the *Tap*pers look familiar!)

To Kill a Mockingbird

This masterpiece offers crucial lessons about prejudice.

Director: Robert Mulligan **Cast:** Gregory Peck, Mary Badham, Phillip Alford
Running time: 129 minutes **Theatrical release date:** 12/25/1962 **Genre:** Drama
MPAA rating: NR

Like Harper Lee's source novel, this perennial favorite is one of Hollywood's most enduring classics. Tackling the issues of racism and prejudice head on, it respects younger viewers' intelligence while simultaneously teaching them important lessons. The 1930s-set story follows Southern lawyer Atticus Finch (Gregory Peck, in his most memorable performance), who defends an African American man accused of raping a white woman. As Atticus works on his case, his children–Scout (Mary Badham) and Jem (Phillip Alford)–learn about tolerance, empathy, and respect. Jem is attacked (mostly off-screen), there are some tense courtroom scenes during the trial, and neighbor Boo Radley (Robert Duvall) seems somewhat scary at first, but what you and your kids will remember most about this movie is its heartfelt messages. After watching, take advantage of the opportunity to talk to your kids about prejudice and the fears that motivate it.

Toy Story

One of the best kids' movies of all time.

on 4+
★★★★★

Director: John Lasseter **Cast:** Tom Hanks, Tim Allen, Don Rickles
Running time: 81 minutes **Theatrical release date:** 11/22/1995 **Genre:** Animated
MPAA rating: G

You don't *have* to be a kid to love *Toy Story*, but this may be the perfect first movie for your child. The first feature film animated entirely by computer, this Pixar release is as charming today as it was when it came out. Hearing the great vocal performances behind rivals/friends Woody and Buzz Lightyear and their gang of fellow toys is like spending a night with old friends. The littlest kids might get a little squirrelly when Buzz is accidentally knocked out of the window, since they can be sensitive about separations. But there's nothing in this movie that they can't handle if they've spent a day on the playground with other children. Happily, *Toy Story 2* is almost as good—so if you get tired of watching this first one over and over with your kids (which they'll want to do), you have an equally good sequel to enjoy.

Walking with Dinosaurs

Dinosaur fans, get ready to snuggle up!

on 9+
★★★★★

Director: Tim Haines, Jasper James **Cast:** Kenneth Branagh **Running time:** 180 minutes **Release date:** 4/16/2000 **Genre:** Documentary **MPAA rating:** NR

Like a straightforward nature documentary, this ambitious production (it originally aired as six separate episodes on the Discovery Channel) combines stunning photography and state-of-the-art digital effects to bring the evolution and demise of the dinosaurs to life in all of their living, howling splendor. Narrated by Kenneth Branagh, the DVD contains additional footage not seen in the original broadcast (you might want to screen it before letting young viewers loose). Although presented in matter-of-fact, scientific fashion, some of the dramatizations may be too much for younger or more sensitive kids, since the dinosaurs are shown attacking and eating each other, as well as peeing and pooping. Sauropods and others are discreetly shown coupled; mating rituals and habits are discussed. But for your dino-lovers, this is dyno-mite.

Wallace and Gromit in Three Amazing Adventures

Witty claymation shorts with whole-family appeal.

on 6+
★★★★★

Director: Nick Park **Cast:** Peter Sallis, Anne Reid **Running time:** 83 minutes **Theatrical release date:** 3/8/1990 **Genre:** Animated **MPAA rating:** NR

This compilation of three award-winning short claymation movies—*A Grand Day Out*, *The Wrong Trousers*, and *A Close Shave*—features hapless British inventor Wallace and his smart, loyal dog companion Gromit. Preschoolers will enjoy lovable-looking Wallace and Gromit but may find certain scenes a bit scary, while elementary school kids will love the slapstick humor and will replay their favorite scenes over and over again. And tweens, teens, and adults will appreciate the brilliant animation, hilarious scripts, great special effects, and impressive action-adventure sequences. In short, this is a must-see trilogy for the whole family. For feature-length Wallace and Gromit fun, try *Wallace and Gromit: The Curse of the Were-Rabbit*.

West Side Story

A masterpiece for families to enjoy together.

ON 11+

★★★★★

Director: Jerome Robbins, Robert Wise **Cast:** Natalie Wood, Rita Moreno, Richard Beymer **Running time:** 152 minutes **Theatrical release date:** 10/18/1961 **Genre:** Musical **MPAA rating:** NR

This beautiful musical take on *Romeo and Juliet* is a visual masterpiece packed with talent. Leonard Bernstein and Stephen Sondheim's music is unforgettable, as are the Oscar-winning performances by George Chakiris as Bernardo and Rita Moreno as Anita, his spunky girlfriend. Because it's a musical, the characters' raging emotions are expressed through song and dance, which is important to remind twelve-year-old viewers who might wonder know why on earth rival gang members are dancing. Even if your kids would rather see the latest action thriller, put this movie on one night and wait five minutes. That's all it will take to enchant them. The biggest problem? Parents may be tempted to sing along–never a good idea when watching with your kids unless you want a ruthless ribbing!

Whale Rider

Excellent to watch and discuss as a family.

Director: Niki Caro **Cast:** Keisha Castle-Hughes, Rawiri Paratene, Vicky Haughton **Running time:** 101 minutes **Theatrical release date:** 7/4/2003 **Genre:** Drama **MPAA rating:** PG-13

According to legend, the Maori came to Whangara when their great leader, Paikea, led them by riding on a whale. Ever since, the Maori have been led by Paikea's male descendants. So when her mother and twin brother (the heir) die in childbirth in a very sad scene, her father leaves newborn daughter Paikea with her grandfather—because Pai (for short) obviously isn't worthy to carry on as a leader in training. But young Pai is determined to prove herself. This lyrical, especially touching film features a fiery performance from Oscar nominee Keisha Castle-Hughes and handles a little-known culture with great dignity. It's a fine choice for tweens who are ready for scenes of tense family confrontation and some drinking, smoking, and a brief drug reference. And it's great for whole families ready for some heartfelt discussions of traditions and gender equality.

Willow

Small hero faces huge challenge to save a baby.

on 8+

Director: Ron Howard **Cast:** Warwick Davis, Val Kilmer, Joanne Whalley **Running time:** 126 minutes **Theatrical release date:** 5/20/1988 **Genre:** Fantasy **MPAA rating:** PG

This magical fantasy penned by George Lucas is perfect for tweens who've already memorized the lines to all of the *Harry Potter* movies. Warwick Davis stars as farmer Willow Ufgood, a member of a dwarf race who desperately wants to be a sorcerer. When his children find a "Daikini" (aka "big person") baby, he becomes a hero instead, saving the baby—who's really a princess—from an evil queen bent on destroying her. Along the way, he has to decide whom to trust, especially when his sword-wielding protector (Val Kilmer) is a convicted criminal who falls for the evil queen's daughter. A few battle scenes get bloody, there are a few scary creatures, and some very tiny sidekicks get rather tipsy, but this good vs. evil tale is filled with adventure and light humor that tweens and older Muggles will definitely enjoy.

Willy Wonka and the Chocolate Factory

Pure, sweet imagination for both kids and adults.

on 8+

★★★★★

Director: Mel Stuart **Cast:** Gene Wilder, Peter Ostrum, Jack Albertson **Running time:** 100 minutes **Theatrical release date:** 6/30/1971 **Genre:** Fantasy **MPAA rating:** G

The Johnny Depp remake is all well and good, but for the real thing, rent this original, fantastical take on Roald Dahl's tale. Here Gene Wilder owns the factory, complete with a chocolate river, test labs full of newfangled treats, and riddling orange Oompa-Loompas. Families will cheer for Charlie when he gets the golden ticket, and parents will enjoy the sardonic humor and the delightful lessons on behavior like gluttony, TV addiction, spoiled brattiness ("I want a golden goose NOOOOW!"), and more–Willy Wonka should guest-star on *Supernanny*! The build-up is slow, with one too many songs, but once kids step inside the chocolate factory, they'll hook their sweet teeth into it. Just watch out for a couple frightening scenes of kids in peril and a rather nightmarish boat ride.

The Wizard of Oz

Family classic will send kids over the rainbow.

on 6+

★★★★★

Director: Victor Fleming **Cast:** Judy Garland, Ray Bolger, Jack Haley **Running time:** 101 minutes **Theatrical release date:** 8/25/1939 **Genre:** Classics **MPAA rating:** G

Ever since Judy Garland first wistfully sang about going "Somewhere over the Rainbow," families have been hooked on this timeless classic. And for good reason: L. Frank Baum's story about a little Kansas girl who's whisked via tornado to a magical land where scarecrows talk and monkeys fly is about as magical as movies get. That said, there are several scenes that might scare younger viewers–that imposing tornado, Miss Gulch transforming into the Wicked Witch of the West, the witch threatening Dorothy and disappearing in clouds of red smoke, the friends being attacked by the trees and the aforementioned monkeys, and so on. Talk to your kids about the story before watching, and watch it with them to gauge their reactions. Then, once they're hooked, expect them to want to see it again and again.

Yellow Submarine

Beatles classic with great animation and even better music.

Director: George Dunning **Cast:** Paul McCartney, John Lennon, George Harrison, Ringo Starr **Running time:** 85 minutes **Theatrical release date:** 11/13/1968 **Genre:** Animated **MPAA rating:** G

All is peace, love, and music in gentle Pepperland–until the wicked Blue Meanies take over. The Beatles come to the rescue via the titular vessel, meeting all kinds of strange and interesting characters along the way. This movie is a pleasure for the eye, ear, and heart, featuring spectacular animation, gorgeous music (including the title song, "When I'm Sixty-four," "Lucy in the Sky with Diamonds," and "All Together Now"), and a sweet story with a nonviolent happy ending. A perfect way to revisit your youth!

Young Frankenstein

Brooks' corniness yields plenty of belly laughs.

on 10+
★★★★★

Director: Mel Brooks **Cast:** Gene Wilder, Peter Boyle, Marty Feldman **Running time:** 106 minutes **Theatrical release date:** 12/15/1974 **Genre:** Comedy **MPAA rating:** PG

Mel Brooks' corny brand of humor meets classic horror cinema in this irresistible parody. Frankenstein's son (Gene Wilder) inherits his father's estate and all the lore that goes with it. Before long, he embraces his destiny, channels some lightning atop the castle (the same one from the classic *Frankenstein*, and voila! A very needy, temperamental monster (Peter Boyle) is ALIVE. Families will be in hysterics as the monster dons a bow-tie and sings "Puttin' on the Ritz." And when he falls for Madeline Kahn (in some scenes that are chock-full of sexual jokes, one just after sex), his life takes a surprisingly yuppie turn. For comedy and horror fans old enough for the bawdiness, this is a must-see.

MOVIES BY TOPIC

Adventures

Goldfinger
Thrilling action comedy may be the best Bond.
on 14+ ★★★★

Raiders of the Lost Ark
A thrill ride and a half.
on 12+ ★★★★★

Star Wars: Episode V: The Empire Strikes Back
They're all great. This is the best of the best.
on 8+ ★★★★★

Swiss Family Robinson
A good introduction for kids reluctant to watch old movies.
on 8+ ★★★★

The Goonies
A classic '80s action-fantasy–tweens will love!
on 10+ ★★★★

Bad Boy Movies

Ferris Bueller's Day Off
Hilarious comedy classic; language makes it PG-13.
on 14+ ★★★★★

The Karate Kid
A classic coming-of-age story that remains fresh.
on 9+ ★★★★

Stand by Me
Edgy coming-of-age story not for young kids.
on 15+ ★★★★

Baseball Movies

Angels in the Outfield
Heartwarming movie about hope and baseball.
on 7+
★★★★

A League of Their Own
Terrific tweens-and-up story of women's baseball.
on 10+
★★★★

The Sandlot
Field of Dreams for tweens.
on 8+
★★★★

Biopics

Amadeus
Great movie. Stupidly R for a naked tush and a bit of hanky-panky.
on 12+
★★★★

Gandhi
Brilliant biography that will engage preteens and up.
on 11+
★★★★★

Lawrence of Arabia
Mature teens will appreciate this gripping epic.
on 13+
★★★★★

Selena
J-Lo hits the right notes in Tejano star's tale.
on 9+
★★★★

Car Movies

Back to the Future
'80s sci-fi time-travel hit offers laughs and romance.
on 8+ ★★★★★

Cars
Pixar comedy is full of four-wheeled fun.
on 5+ ★★★★

Chitty Chitty Bang Bang
A car story custom made for kids.
on 6+ ★★★★

Classic Comedies

The Absent-Minded Professor
Family entertainment at its best.
on 6+ ★★★★★

Modern Times
Families will cherish Chaplin's silent slapstick.
on 6+ ★★★★★

Monty Python and the Holy Grail
Nonstop hilarity for families; some bawdy humor.
on 13+ ★★★★★

The Return of the Pink Panther
Hilarious Inspector Clouseau better in this sequel than the original.
on 10+ ★★★★

Some Like It Hot
One of the wildest farces ever.
on 11+ ★★★★★

Young Frankenstein
Brooks' corniness yields plenty of belly laughs.
on 10+ ★★★★★

Classic Sports Movies

Title	Description	Age	Rating
Breaking Away	Rousing bicycle race story is a family favorite.	on 10+	★★★★
Chariots of Fire	Brilliant true story of 1924 Olympic footrace.	on 10+	★★★★★
Hoosiers	A tale of heroic sportsmanship.	on 9+	★★★★★

Classics Worth Making Your Kids Watch

Title	Description	Age	Rating
Casablanca	Every kid should see this Bogart classic.	on 10+	★★★★★
Dr. Strangelove, or: How I Stopped Worrying and Learned to Love the Bomb	Classic Kubrick black comedy for smart teens and up.	on 14+	★★★★★
Gone with the Wind	We know it, we love it, even fifty-plus years later.	on 10+	★★★★★
Lawrence of Arabia	Mature teens will appreciate this gripping epic.	on 13+	★★★★★
Singin' in the Rain	This is often considered the finest musical of all time.	on 6+	★★★★★
Some Like It Hot	One of the wildest farces ever.	on 11+	★★★★★
To Kill a Mockingbird	This masterpiece offers crucial lessons about prejudice.	on 12+	★★★★★

Coming-of-Age

Big
Wonderful story with some mature material.
on 12+ ★★★★

Billy Elliot
Terrific story of a young boy ballet dancer.
on 14+ ★★★★

Dead Poets Society
Robin Williams in dramatic role as teacher to troubled boys.
on 13+ ★★★★

Fly Away Home
Thrilling, touching adventure for animal lovers.
on 8+ ★★★★★

The Lion King
Disney's tuneful king-of-the-beasts blockbuster.
on 5+ ★★★★

Stand by Me
Edgy coming-of-age story not for young kids.
on 15+ ★★★★

Dance Movies

Billy Elliot
Terrific story of a young boy ballet dancer.
on 14+ ★★★★

Mad Hot Ballroom
Dance documentary hits all the right beats.
on 8+ ★★★★★

West Side Story
A masterpiece for families to enjoy together.
on 11+ ★★★★★

Documentaries

Hoop Dreams
Stunning documentary, great family viewing with older kids.
on 14+ ★★★★★

Mad Hot Ballroom
Dance documentary hits all the right beats.
on 8+ ★★★★★

March of the Penguins
The penguin movie. A stunning, loving documentary.
on 6+ ★★★★★

Spellbound
Every family should see this m-a-r-v-e-l-o-u-s movie.
on 10+ ★★★★★

Walking with Dinosaurs
Dinosaur fans, get ready to snuggle up!
on 9+ ★★★★★

Dog Movies

101 Dalmatians
Lovable cartoon classic for all ages.
on 5+ ★★★★★

Homeward Bound: The Incredible Journey
This adventurous animal tale will have kids riveted.
on 5+ ★★★★

March of the Penguins
The penguin movie. A stunning, loving documentary.
on 6+ ★★★★★

Lady and the Tramp
Classic Disney dogs paw their way into kids' hearts.
on 5+ ★★★★★

Old Yeller
Tearjerker is one of the best early Disney dramas.
on 8+ ★★★★★

Wallace and Gromit in Three Amazing Adventures
Witty claymation shorts with whole-family appeal.
on 6+ ★★★★★

Fairy-Tale Movies

Beauty and the Beast
You can't judge a beast by his cupboard.
on 5+ ★★★★★

Cinderella
Sweet fairy-tale classic for little princesses.
on 5+ ★★★★★

Shrek
Gross-out laughs meet a marvelous fairy-tale mix.
on 6+ ★★★★★

Snow White and the Seven Dwarfs
Still a delight, with memorable songs and characters.
on 4+ ★★★★☆

The Princess Bride
Witty, winsome fairy tale for the whole family.
on 8+ ★★★★★

Family Musicals

Annie
Tale of cute orphan is great for the whole family.
on 6+ ★★★★★

Fiddler on the Roof
Epic portrait of Jewish life during the Russian Revolution.
on 10+ ★★★★★

Grease
Musical phenomenon is great fun but racy.
on 13+ ★★★★☆

Mary Poppins
World's coolest nanny celebrates family and fun.
on 6+ ★★★★★

Moulin Rouge
Dazzling musical romance for teens.
on 15+ ★★★★☆

The Music Man
Glorious production, with gorgeous music, dancing.
on 6+ ★★★★★

My Fair Lady
Tuneful, witty, stylish musical to entertain all ages.
on 6+ ★★★★★

Oliver!
Glorious musical based on *Oliver Twist*.
on 8+ ★★★★

Singin' in the Rain
This is often considered the finest musical of all time.
on 6+ ★★★★★

The Sound of Music
Outstanding family film features glorious music.
on 6+ ★★★★★

West Side Story
A masterpiece for families to enjoy together.
on 11+ ★★★★★

The Wizard of Oz
Family classic will send kids over the rainbow.
on 6+ ★★★★★

Fantasy Worlds

The Chronicles of Narnia: The Lion, the Witch, and the Wardrobe
Timeless classic faithfully rendered.
on 9+ ★★★★

The Dark Crystal
A fantastic but more intense Muppet adventure.
on 7+ ★★★★

The Lord of the Rings: The Fellowship of the Ring
Fabulous, but also violent and scary.
on 12+ ★★★★★

The NeverEnding Story
A book-loving boy gets caught up in his own fantasy tale.
on 8+ ★★★★

The Secret of NIMH
Fascinating, but sensitive animal-lovers beware.
on 8+ ★★★★

Willow
Small hero faces huge challenge to save a baby.
on 8+ ★★★★

The Wizard of Oz
Family classic will send kids over the rainbow.
on 6+ ★★★★★

Father-Son Stories

The Lion King
Disney's tuneful king-of-the-beasts blockbuster.
on 5+ ★★★★

Billy Elliot
Terrific story of a young boy ballet dancer.
on 14+ ★★★★

Finding Nemo
Sweet father-son tale is perfect family viewing.
on 4+ ★★★★★

Adventures

The Brave Little Toaster
Appliances make a suspenseful, incredible journey.
on 5+ ★★★★

Finding Nemo
Sweet father-son tale is perfect family viewing.
on 4+ ★★★★★

The Land before Time
Baby dinosaur buddy flick that started the series.
on 4+ ★★★★

Mary Poppins
World's coolest nanny celebrates family and fun.
on 6+ ★★★★★

The Muppet Movie
Classic first big-screen outing for Jim Henson's Muppets.
on 5+ ★★★★

Snow White and the Seven Dwarfs
Still a delight, with memorable songs and characters.
on 4+ ★★★★

Foreign Films

Howl's Moving Castle
Charming Miyazaki fairy tale appeals to boys and girls equally.
on 9+ ★★★★

My Neighbor Totoro
One of the best family movies of all time.
on 5+ ★★★★★

Spirited Away
Magnificent, spellbinding movie with a bit of an edge.
on 10+ ★★★★★

Cinema Paradiso
Charming Italian film about friendship, movies.
on 13+ ★★★★

Crouching Tiger, Hidden Dragon
Amazing martial arts fairy tale. Magisterial and magical.
on 12+ ★★★★★

Great African American Movies

Movie	Age	Rating
Akeelah and the Bee Inspiring drama about a champion speller.	on 8+	★★★★☆
Barbershop Charming urban comedy for teens.	on 13+	★★★★☆
The Color Purple Inspiring, sentimental tale of survival.	on 14+	★★★★★
Drumline Outstanding cast, great message, strong language.	on 11+	★★★★☆

Great Classic, Great Remake

Movie	Age	Rating
101 Dalmatians Lovable cartoon classic for all ages.	on 5+	★★★★★
The Absent-Minded Professor Family entertainment at its best.	on 6+	★★★★★
Doctor Dolittle Animal-friendly, kid-friendly classic.	on 5+	★★★★☆
Freaky Friday Mother-daughter switch is fun comedic chaos.	on 8+	★★★★☆
Little Women Alcott adaptation tugs at your heartstrings.	on 11+	★★★★☆
Miracle on 34th Street Classic holiday movie for the whole family.	on 6+	★★★★☆

The Parent Trap
Hayley Mills rocks in her dual role as twins.
on 6+
★★★★

Willy Wonka and the Chocolate Factory
Pure, sweet imagination for both kids and adults.
on 8+
★★★★★

Great Latino Movies

Real Women Have Curves
Ugly Betty star captivates in teen drama.
on 14+
★★★★★

Selena
J-Lo hits the right notes in Tejano star's tale.
on 9+
★★★★

Spy Kids
Just the right combination of fantasy and comedy.
on 7+
★★★★

West Side Story
A masterpiece for families to enjoy together.
on 11+
★★★★★

Holiday Movies

A Charlie Brown Christmas
The Peanuts gang in a classic Christmas special.
on 2+
★★★★★

A Christmas Story
Wonderful antidote to saccharine holiday stories.
on 8+
★★★★★

Dr. Seuss' How the Grinch Stole Christmas
Heartwarming TV special true to Seuss' classic.
on 4+
★★★★★

Elf
Peppy holiday favorite for both kids and parents.
on 7+
★★★★

Home Alone
Slapstick family comedy is a modern holiday classic.
on 7+ ★★★★

It's a Wonderful Life
This classic delivers warmth all year long.
on 9+ ★★★★★

Miracle on 34th Street
Classic holiday movie for the whole family.
on 6+ ★★★★

Literary Classics (Book-to-Screen)

Alice in Wonderland
Surreal Disney classic with wild-card characters.
on 4+ ★★★★

Charlotte's Web
Enchanting take on a beloved children's classic.
on 5+ ★★★★★

The Color Purple
Inspiring, sentimental tale of survival.
on 14+ ★★★★★

The Chronicles of Narnia: The Lion, the Witch, and the Wardrobe
Timeless classic faithfully rendered.
on 9+ ★★★★

Harry Potter and the Sorcerer's Stone
First Potter movie is a big-budget magical ride.
on 7+ ★★★★★

Holes
Great movie respects its audience's intelligence.
on 10+ ★★★★

Indian in the Cupboard
Classic, heartwarming fantasy will rivet kids.
on 6+ ★★★★★

James and the Giant Peach
Fabulous adaptation of Roald Dahl's classic book.
on 7+ ★★★★

A Little Princess O
Wonderful movie of a lonely girl's triumph.
on 7+ ★★★★

Little Women
Alcott adaptation tugs at your heartstrings.
on 11+ ★★★★

The Lord of the Rings: The Fellowship of the Ring
Fabulous, but also violent and scary. **On for 12+ 5*s**
on 12+ ★★★★★

The NeverEnding Story On for 8+ 4*s
A book-loving boy gets caught up in his own fantasy tale.
on 8+ ★★★★

Of Mice and Men
An elegant adaptation of Steinbeck's classic Depression-era novel.
on 13+ ★★★★★

Old Yeller
Tearjerker is one of the best early Disney dramas.
on 8+ ★★★★★

The Pagemaster
An entertaining film little kids will enjoy, full of positive messages.
on 5+ ★★★★

Pride and Prejudice
Gorgeous Jane Austen adaptation.
on 10+ ★★★★

The Princess Bride
Witty, winsome fairy tale for the whole family.
on 8+ ★★★★★

The Secret of NIMH
Fascinating, but sensitive animal-lovers beware.
on 8+ ★★★★

Shrek
Gross-out laughs meet a marvelous fairy-tale mix.
on 6+ ★★★★★

Swiss Family Robinson
A good introduction for kids reluctant to watch old movies.
on 8+ ★★★★

To Kill a Mockingbird
This masterpiece offers crucial lessons about prejudice.
on 12+ ★★★★★

Willy Wonka and the Chocolate Factory
Pure, sweet imagination for both kids and adults.
on 8+ ★★★★★

The Wizard of Oz
Family classic will send kids over the rainbow.
on 6+ ★★★★★

Magical Movies

Aladdin
A magic carpet ride of a movie from Disney.
on 6+ ★★★★★

Fantasia
A breathtaking animation feat.
on 5+ ★★★★★

Harry Potter and the Sorcerer's Stone
First Potter movie is a big-budget magical ride.
on 7+ ★★★★★

Willow
Small hero faces huge challenge to save a baby.
on 8+ ★★★★

The Pagemaster
An entertaining film little kids will enjoy, full of positive messages.
on 5+ ★★★★

The Sword in the Stone
Delightful classic brings Arthur legend to life.
on 5+ ★★★★

Meaning-of-Life Lessons

Groundhog Day
A witty, sarcastic take on redemption.
on 10+ ★★★★★

It's a Wonderful Life
This classic delivers warmth all year long.
on 9+ ★★★★★

Mrs. Doubtfire
You'll laugh, you'll cry. Best divorce movie.
on 12+ ★★★★

The Lion King
Disney's tuneful king-of-the-beasts blockbuster.
on 5+ ★★★★

Mother-Daughter Stories

Little Women
Alcott adaptation tugs at your heartstrings.
on 11+ ★★★★

The Princess Diaries
Terrific fun for girls and their families, too.
on 6+ ★★★★★

Freaky Friday
Mother-daughter switch is fun comedic chaos.
on 8+ ★★★★

(Not Too) Scary Movies

Title	Description	Rating	Age
The Dark Crystal	A fantastic but more intense Muppet adventure.	★★★★	on 7+
E.T. the Extra-Terrestrial	Touching family classic is still one of the best.	★★★★★	on 7+
Ghostbusters	Paranormal fun for the whole family.	★★★★	on 10+
The Goonies	A classic '80s action-fantasy–tweens will love!	★★★★	on 10+
Harry Potter and the Sorcerer's Stone	First Potter movie is a big-budget magical ride.	★★★★★	on 7+
Monsters, Inc.	Cuddly, adorable, kid-friendly monster movie.	★★★★	on 5+
The Nightmare before Christmas	Tim Burton magic with just a touch of scariness.	★★★★★	on 6+

Offbeat Gems

Title	Description	Rating	Age
Alice in Wonderland	Surreal Disney classic with wild-card characters.	★★★★	on 4+
Edward Scissorhands	Dark yet sweet underdog tale for older kids.	★★★★	on 13+
James and the Giant Peach	Fabulous adaptation of Roald Dahl's classic book.	★★★★	on 7+
Monty Python and the Holy Grail	Nonstop hilarity for families; some bawdy humor.	★★★★★	on 13+

Napoleon Dynamite
One-of-a-kind high school comedy for the family.
on 11+ ★★★★

The Nightmare before Christmas
Tim Burton magic with just a touch of scariness.
on 6+ ★★★★★

Pee-wee's Big Adventure
Just as charming and curious as it was in 1985.
on 6+ ★★★★

The Princess Bride
Witty, winsome fairy tale for the whole family.
on 8+ ★★★★★

Willy Wonka and the Chocolate Factory
Pure, sweet imagination for both kids and adults.
on 8+ ★★★★★

Yellow Submarine
Beatles classic with great animation and even better music.
on 7+ ★★★★★

Pirate Movies

Pirates of the Caribbean: The Curse of the Black Pearl
Rip-roaring fun for kids who don't mind skeletons.
on 12+ ★★★★

Swiss Family Robinson
A good introduction for kids reluctant to watch old movies.
on 8+ ★★★★

The Goonies
A classic '80s action-fantasy–tweens will love!
on 10+ ★★★★

Rock and Roll Movies

American Graffiti
Coming-of-age classic still a must-see for teens.
on 13+
★★★★★

Grease
Musical phenomenon is great fun but racy.
on 11+
★★★★

A Hard Day's Night
Beatles classic holds up as fabulously as the Fab Four.
on 8+
★★★★★

Moulin Rouge
Dazzling musical romance for teens.
on 15+
★★★★

School of Rock
Standout Jack Black in hilarious nerd-becomes-cool comedy.
on 12+
★★★★

This is Spinal Tap
Hilarious, ribald, drug-filled rock send-up.
on 14+
★★★★

Yellow Submarine
Beatles classic with great animation and even better music.
on 7+
★★★★★

Sleepover Movies

Clueless
Charming, funny take on Jane Austen's *Emma*.
on 14+
★★★★

Ferris Bueller's Day Off
Hilarious comedy classic; language makes it PG-13.
on 14+
★★★★★

Grease
Musical phenomenon is great fun but racy.
on 13+
★★★★

Mean Girls Mature but often hilarious teen comedy.	on 14+ ★★★★
Moulin Rouge Dazzling musical romance for teens.	on 15+ ★★★★
My Big Fat Greek Wedding The perfect sleepover movie for tween girls (and their moms, too!)	on 12+ ★★★★
The Sisterhood of the Traveling Pants Sensitive portrayal of four girls' friendships.	on 11+ ★★★★

Space Movies

2001: A Space Odyssey Kubrick's sci-fi masterpiece is still relevant.	on 12+ ★★★★★
E.T. the Extra-Terrestrial Touching family classic is still one of the best.	on 7+ ★★★★★
Spaceballs Goofy parody mocks the *Star Wars* series.	on 11+ ★★★★
Star Wars: Episode V: The Empire Strikes Back They're all great. This is the best of the best.	on 8+ ★★★★★

Sports Movies

A League of Their Own
Terrific tweens-and-up story of women's baseball.
on 10+ ★★★★

Bend It Like Beckham
Superb rendering of a girl's struggle to do what she loves.
on 13+ ★★★★

Hoop Dreams
Stunning documentary, great family viewing with older kids.
on 14+ ★★★★★

Remember the Titans
Inspiring football drama brings history to life.
on 8+ ★★★★

Rudy
Inspiring sports film about a real life underdog.
on 9+ ★★★★★

The Karate Kid
A classic coming-of-age story that remains fresh.
on 9+ ★★★★

The Sandlot
Field of Dreams for tweens.
on 8+ ★★★★

Starring Live Animals

Babe
Heartwarming farm tale is touching–and a bit scary.
on 5+ ★★★★★

Charlotte's Web
Enchanting take on a beloved children's classic.
on 5+ ★★★★★

Homeward Bound: The Incredible Journey
This adventurous animal tale will have kids riveted.
on 5+ ★★★★

Old Yeller
Tearjerker is one of the best early Disney dramas.
on 8+ ★★★★★

The Adventures of Milo and Otis
A lovable pet tale.
on 5+ ★★★★★

Strong Girls

A League of Their Own
Terrific tweens-and-up story of women's baseball.
on 10+ ★★★★

A Little Princess
Wonderful movie of a lonely girl's triumph.
on 7+ ★★★★

Akeelah and the Bee
Inspiring drama about a champion speller.
on 8+ ★★★★

Annie
Tale of cute orphan is great for the whole family.
on 6+ ★★★★★

Bend It Like Beckham
Superb rendering of a girl's struggle to do what she loves.
on 13+ ★★★★

Mulan
Disneyfied but dignified tale of Chinese warrior.
on 5+ ★★★★

The Princess Diaries
Terrific fun for girls and their families, too.
on 6+ ★★★★★

Real Women Have Curves
Ugly Betty star captivates in teen drama.
on 14+ ★★★★★

Selena
J-Lo hits the right notes in Tejano star's tale.
on 9+ ★★★★

Whale Rider
Excellent to watch and discuss as a family.
on 11+ ★★★★

Superhero Movies

Batman Begins
Smart and entertaining, but also very violent.
on 13+ ★★★★

The Incredibles
Incredible! But action too much for youngest kids.
on 7+ ★★★★★

Spider-Man
A fun movie; may be too intense for younger kids.
on 11+ ★★★★

Superman: The Movie
Super-nostalgic adventure still soars.
on 8+ ★★★★

Talking about Loss

Bambi
Disney's original circle-of-life story.
on 5+ ★★★★★

Dead Poets Society
Robin Williams in dramatic role as teacher to troubled boys.
on 13+ ★★★★

The Lion King
Disney's tuneful king-of-the-beasts blockbuster.
on 5+ ★★★★

Old Yeller
Tearjerker is one of the best early Disney dramas.
on 8+ ★★★★★

Triumph of the Underdogs

Title	Description	Age	Rating
The Goonies	A classic '80s action-fantasy–tweens will love!	on 10+	★★★★☆
Rudy	Inspiring sports film about a real life underdog.	on 9+	★★★★★
The Sandlot	*Field of Dreams* for tweens.	on 8+	★★★★☆
Stand by Me	Edgy coming-of-age story not for young kids.	on 15+	★★★★☆

MOVIES BY GENRE

Action/Adventure

Batman Begins
Smart and entertaining, but also very violent.
on 13+ ★★★★

Crouching Tiger, Hidden Dragon
Amazing martial arts fairy tale. Magisterial and magical.
on 12+ ★★★★★

Goldfinger
Thrilling action comedy may be the best Bond.
on 14+ ★★★★

The Goonies
A classic '80s action-fantasy—tweens will love!
on 10+ ★★★★

Homeward Bound: The Incredible Journey
This adventurous animal tale will have kids riveted.
on 5+ ★★★★

North by Northwest
Witty thriller from the master of suspense, Alfred Hitchcock.
on 11+ ★★★★

Pirates of the Caribbean: The Curse of the Black Pearl
Rip-roaring fun for kids who don't mind skeletons.
on 12+ ★★★★

Raiders of the Lost Ark
A thrill ride and a half.
on 12+ ★★★★★

Spider-Man
A fun movie; may be too intense for younger kids.
on 11+ ★★★★

Spy Kids
Just the right combination of fantasy and comedy.
on 7+ ★★★★

Star Wars: Episode V: The Empire Strikes Back
They're all great. This is the best of the best.
on 8+ ★★★★★

Superman: The Movie
Super-nostalgic adventure still soars.
on 8+ ★★★★

Swiss Family Robinson
A good introduction for kids reluctant to watch old movies.
on 8+ ★★★★

Animated

101 Dalmatians
Lovable cartoon classic for all ages.
on 5+ ★★★★★

Aladdin
A magic carpet ride of a movie from Disney.
on 6+ ★★★★★

Alice in Wonderland
Surreal Disney classic with wild-card characters.
on 4+ ★★★★

Bambi
Disney's original circle-of-life story.
on 5+ ★★★★★

Beauty and the Beast
You can't judge a beast by his cupboard.
on 5+ ★★★★★

The Brave Little Toaster
Appliances make a suspenseful, incredible journey.
on 5+ ★★★★

Cars
Pixar comedy is full of four-wheeled fun.
on 5+ ★★★★

A Charlie Brown Christmas
The Peanuts gang in a classic Christmas special.
on 2+ ★★★★★

Chicken Run
Fabulous animation from Wallace and Gromit creator.
on 6+ ★★★★

Cinderella
Sweet fairy-tale classic for little princesses.
on 5+ ★★★★★

Dr. Seuss' How the Grinch Stole Christmas!
Heartwarming TV special true to Seuss' classic.
on 4+ ★★★★★

Fantasia
A breathtaking animation feat.
on 5+ ★★★★★

Finding Nemo
Sweet father-son tale is perfect family viewing.
on 4+ ★★★★★

Howl's Moving Castle
Charming Miyazaki fairy tale appeals to boys and girls equally.
on 9+ ★★★★

The Incredibles
Incredible! But action too much for youngest kids.
on 7+ ★★★★★

The Iron Giant
A director's cut re-release of a wonderful family movie.
on 5+ ★★★★

James and the Giant Peach
Fabulous adaptation of Roald Dahl's classic book.
on 7+ ★★★★

Lady and the Tramp
Classic Disney dogs paw their way into kids' hearts.
on 5+ ★★★★★

The Land before Time
Baby dinosaur buddy flick that started the series.
on 4+ ★★★★

The Lion King
Disney's tuneful king-of-the-beasts blockbuster.
on 5+ ★★★★

The Little Mermaid
A superbly entertaining animated musical.
on 6+ ★★★★★

Title	Description	Rating	Age	Stars
Monsters, Inc.	Cuddly, adorable, kid-friendly monster movie.	on	5+	★★★★
Mulan	Disneyfied but dignified tale of Chinese warrior.	on	5+	★★★★
My Neighbor Totoro	One of the best family movies of all time.	on	5+	★★★★★
The Nightmare before Christmas	Tim Burton magic with just a touch of scariness.	on	6+	★★★★★
The Secret of NIMH	Fascinating, but sensitive animal-lovers beware.	on	8+	★★★★
Shrek	Gross-out laughs meet a marvelous fairy-tale mix.	on	6+	★★★★★
Snow White and the Seven Dwarfs	Still a delight, with memorable songs and characters.	on	4+	★★★★
Spirited Away	Magnificent, spellbinding movie with a bit of an edge.	on	10+	★★★★★
The Sword in the Stone	Delightful classic brings Arthur legend to life.	on	5+	★★★★
Toy Story	One of the best kids' movies of all time.	on	4+	★★★★
Wallace and Gromit in Three Amazing Adventures	Witty claymation shorts with whole-family appeal.	on	6+	★★★★★
Yellow Submarine	Beatles classic with great animation and even better music.	on	7+	★★★★★

Classics

Title	Description	Age	Rating
Casablanca	Every kid should see this Bogart classic.	on 10+	★★★★★
Chitty Chitty Bang Bang	A car story custom made for kids.	on 6+	★★★★
Doctor Dolittle	Animal-friendly, kid-friendly classic.	on 5+	★★★★
Gone with the Wind	We know it, we love it, even fifty-plus years later.	on 10+	★★★★★
Lawrence of Arabia	Mature teens will appreciate this gripping epic.	on 13+	★★★★★
Miracle on 34th Street	Classic holiday movie for the whole family.	on 6+	★★★★
Modern Times	Families will cherish Chaplin's silent slapstick.	on 6+	★★★★★
Roman Holiday	A delightful classic in romantic Rome.	on 8+	★★★★★
The Wizard of Oz	Family classic will send kids over the rainbow.	on 6+	★★★★★

Comedy

Title	Description	Age	Rating
The Absent-Minded Professor	Family entertainment at its best.	on 6+	★★★★★
American Graffiti	Coming-of-age classic still a must-see for teens.	on 13+	★★★★★
Angels in the Outfield	Heartwarming movie about hope and baseball.	on 7+	★★★★
Barbershop	Charming urban comedy for teens.	on 13+	★★★★
Bend It Like Beckham	Superb rendering of a girl's struggle to do what she loves.	on 13+	★★★★
Big	Wonderful story with some mature material.	on 12+	★★★★
Breaking Away	Rousing bicycle race story is a family favorite.	on 10+	★★★★
A Christmas Story	Wonderful antidote to saccharine holiday stories.	on 8+	★★★★★
Clueless	Charming, funny take on Jane Austen's *Emma*.	on 14+	★★★★
Dr. Strangelove, or: How I Learned to Stop Worrying and Love the Bomb	Classic Kubrick black comedy for smart teens and up.	on 14+	★★★★★
Elf	Peppy holiday favorite for both kids and parents.	on 7+	★★★★

Ferris Bueller's Day Off
Hilarious comedy classic; language makes it PG-13.
on 14+ ★★★★★

Freaky Friday
Mother-daughter switch is fun comedic chaos.
on 8+ ★★★★

Ghostbusters
Paranormal fun for the whole family.
on 10+ ★★★★

Groundhog Day
A witty, sarcastic take on redemption.
on 10+ ★★★★★

Home Alone
Slapstick family comedy is a modern holiday classic.
on 7+ ★★★★

A League of Their Own
Terrific tweens-and-up story of women's baseball.
on 10+ ★★★★

Mean Girls
Mature but often hilarious teen comedy.
on 14+ ★★★★

Monty Python and the Holy Grail
Nonstop hilarity for families; some bawdy humor.
on 13+ ★★★★★

Mrs. Doubtfire
You'll laugh, you'll cry. Best divorce movie.
on 12+ ★★★★

My Big Fat Greek Wedding
The perfect sleepover movie for tween girls (and their moms, too!)
on 12+ ★★★★

Napoleon Dynamite
One-of-a-kind high school comedy for the family.
on 11+ ★★★★

A Night at the Opera
Marx Brothers masterpiece is still hilarious.
on 8+ ★★★★★

Title	Rating	Age	Stars
The Parent Trap Hayley Mills rocks in her dual role as twins.	on	6+	★★★★
Pee-wee's Big Adventure Just as charming and curious as it was in 1985.	on	6+	★★★★
The Return of the Pink Panther Hilarious Inspector Clouseau better in this sequel than the original.	on	10+	★★★★
The Princess Bride Witty, winsome fairy tale for the whole family.	on	8+	★★★★★
The Princess Diaries **Terrific fun for girls and their families, too.**	on	6+	★★★★★
The Sandlot *Field of Dreams* for tweens.	on	8+	★★★★
The School of Rock Standout Jack Black in hilarious nerd-becomes-cool comedy.	on	12+	★★★★
Some Like It Hot One of the wildest farces ever.	on	11+	★★★★★
Spaceballs Goofy parody mocks the *Star Wars* series.	on	11+	★★★★
This Is Spinal Tap Hilarious, ribald, drug-filled rock send-up.	on	14+	★★★★
Young Frankenstein Brooks' corniness yields plenty of belly laughs.	on	10+	★★★★★

Documentary

Hoop Dreams
Stunning documentary, great family viewing with older kids.
on 14+ ★★★★★

Mad Hot Ballroom
Dance documentary hits all the right beats.
on 8+ ★★★★★

March of the Penguins
The penguin movie. A stunning, loving documentary.
on 6+ ★★★★★

Spellbound
Every family should see this m-a-r-v-e-l-o-u-s movie.
on 10+ ★★★★★

Walking with Dinosaurs
Dinosaur fans, get ready to snuggle up!
on 9+ ★★★★★

Drama

The Adventures of Milo and Otis
A lovable pet tale.
on 5+ ★★★★★

Akeelah and the Bee
Inspiring drama about a champion speller.
on 8+ ★★★★

Amadeus
Great movie. Stupidly R for a naked tush and a bit of hanky-panky.
on 12+ ★★★★

Babe
Heartwarming farm tale is touching–and a bit scary.
on 5+ ★★★★★

Billy Elliot
Terrific story of a young boy ballet dancer.
on 14+ ★★★★

Chariots of Fire
Brilliant true story of 1924 Olympic footrace.
on 10+ ★★★★★

Charlotte's Web
Enchanting take on a beloved children's classic.
on 5+ ★★★★★

Cinema Paradiso
Charming Italian film about friendship, movies.
on 13+ ★★★★

The Color Purple
Inspiring, sentimental tale of survival.
on 14+ ★★★★★

Dead Poets Society
Robin Williams in dramatic role as teacher to troubled boys.
on 13+ ★★★★

Drumline
Outstanding cast, great message, strong language.
on 11+ ★★★★

Fly Away Home
Thrilling, touching adventure for animal lovers.
on 8+ ★★★★★

Holes
Great movie respects its audience's intelligence.
on 10+ ★★★★

Hoosiers
A tale of heroic sportsmanship.
on 9+ ★★★★★

It's a Wonderful Life
This classic delivers warmth all year long.
on 9+ ★★★★★

The Karate Kid
A classic coming-of-age story that remains fresh.
on 9+ ★★★★

Little Women
Alcott adaptation tugs at your heartstrings.
on 11+ ★★★★

Of Mice and Men
An elegant adaptation of Steinbeck's classic Depression-era novel.
on 13+ ★★★★★

Old Yeller
Tearjerker is one of the best early Disney dramas.
on 8+ ★★★★★

Pride and Prejudice
Gorgeous Jane Austen adaptation.
on 10+ ★★★★

Real Women Have Curves
Ugly Betty star captivates in teen drama.
on 14+ ★★★★★

Remember the Titans
Inspiring football drama brings history to life.
on 8+ ★★★★

Rudy
Inspiring sports film about a real life underdog.
on 9+ ★★★★★

Selena
J-Lo hits the right notes in Tejano star's tale.
on 9+ ★★★★

The Sisterhood of the Traveling Pants
Sensitive portrayal of four girls' friendships.
on 11+ ★★★★

Stand by Me
Edgy coming-of-age story not for young kids.
on 15+ ★★★★

To Kill a Mockingbird
This masterpiece offers crucial lessons about prejudice.
on 12+ ★★★★★

Whale Rider
Excellent to watch and discuss as a family.
on 11+ ★★★★

Fantasy

Title	Age	Rating
The Chronicles of Narnia: The Lion, the Witch, and the Wardrobe Timeless classic faithfully rendered.	on 9+	★★★★
The Dark Crystal A fantastic but more intense Muppet adventure.	on 7+	★★★★
Edward Scissorhands Dark yet sweet underdog tale for older kids.	on 13+	★★★★
Harry Potter and the Sorcerer's Stone First Potter movie is a big-budget magical ride.	on 7+	★★★★★
The Indian in the Cupboard Classic, heartwarming fantasy will rivet kids.	on 6+	★★★★★
A Little Princess Wonderful movie of a lonely girl's triumph.	on 7+	★★★★
The Lord of the Rings: The Fellowship of the Ring Fabulous, but also violent and scary.	on 12+	★★★★★
The NeverEnding Story A book-loving boy gets caught up in his own fantasy tale.	on 8+	★★★★
The Pagemaster An entertaining film little kids will enjoy, full of positive messages.	on 5+	★★★★
Willow Small hero faces huge challenge to save a baby.	on 8+	★★★★
Willy Wonka and the Chocolate Factory Pure, sweet imagination for both kids and adults.	on 8+	★★★★★

Musical

Annie
Tale of cute orphan is great for the whole family.
on 6+ ★★★★★

Fiddler on the Roof
Epic portrait of Jewish life during the Russian Revolution.
on 10+ ★★★★★

Grease
Musical phenomenon is great fun but racy.
on 13+ ★★★★☆

A Hard Day's Night
Beatles classic holds up as fabulously as the Fab Four.
on 8+ ★★★★★

Mary Poppins
World's coolest nanny celebrates family and fun.
on 6+ ★★★★★

Moulin Rouge
Dazzling musical romance for teens.
on 15+ ★★★★☆

The Music Man
Glorious production, with gorgeous music, dancing.
on 6+ ★★★★★

My Fair Lady
Tuneful, witty, stylish musical to entertain all ages.
on 6+ ★★★★★

Oliver!
Glorious musical based on *Oliver Twist*.
on 8+ ★★★★☆

Singin' in the Rain
This is often considered the finest musical of all time.
on 6+ ★★★★★

The Sound of Music
Outstanding family film features glorious music.
on 6+ ★★★★★

West Side Story
A masterpiece for families to enjoy together.
on 11+ ★★★★★

Science Fiction

2001: A Space Odyssey — on 12+ ★★★★★
Kubrick's sci-fi masterpiece is still relevant.

Back to the Future — on 8+ ★★★★★
'80s sci-fi time-travel hit offers laughs and romance.

E.T. the Extra-Terrestrial — on 7+ ★★★★★
Touching family classic is still one of the best.

MOVIES BY AGE AND STAGE

Preschool and Kindergarten (2-5)

A Charlie Brown Christmas
The Peanuts gang in a classic Christmas special.
on 2+ ★★★★★

Alice in Wonderland
Surreal Disney classic with wild-card characters.
on 4+ ★★★★

Dr. Seuss' How the Grinch Stole Christmas!
Heartwarming TV special true to Seuss' classic.
on 4+ ★★★★★

Finding Nemo
Sweet father-son tale is perfect family viewing.
on 4+ ★★★★★

The Land before Time
Baby dinosaur buddy flick that started the series.
on 4+ ★★★★

Snow White and the Seven Dwarfs
Still a delight, with memorable songs and characters.
on 4+ ★★★★

Toy Story
One of the best kids' movies of all time.
on 4+ ★★★★

101 Dalmatians
Lovable cartoon classic for all ages.
on 5+ ★★★★★

The Adventures of Milo and Otis
A lovable pet tale.
on 5+ ★★★★★

Babe
Heartwarming farm tale is touching–and a bit scary.
on 5+ ★★★★★

Bambi
Disney's original circle-of-life story.
on 5+ ★★★★★

Beauty and the Beast
You can't judge a beast by his cupboard.
on 5+ ★★★★★

The Brave Little Toaster
Appliances make a suspenseful, incredible journey.
on 5+ ★★★★

Cars
Pixar comedy is full of four-wheeled fun.
on 5+ ★★★★

Charlotte's Web
Enchanting take on a beloved children's classic.
on 5+ ★★★★★

Cinderella
Sweet fairy-tale classic for little princesses.
on 5+ ★★★★★

Doctor Dolittle
Animal-friendly, kid-friendly classic.
on 5+ ★★★★

Fantasia
A breathtaking animation feat.
on 5+ ★★★★★

Homeward Bound: The Incredible Journey
This adventurous animal tale will have kids riveted.
on 5+ ★★★★

The Iron Giant
A director's cut re-release of a wonderful family movie.
on 5+ ★★★★

Lady and the Tramp
Classic Disney dogs paw their way into kids' hearts.
on 5+ ★★★★★

The Lion King
Disney's tuneful king-of-the-beasts blockbuster.
on 5+ ★★★★

Monsters, Inc.
Cuddly, adorable, kid-friendly monster movie.
on 5+ ★★★★

Mulan
Disneyfied but dignified tale of Chinese warrior.
on 5+ ★★★★

My Neighbor Totoro
One of the best family movies of all time.
on 5+ ★★★★★

The Pagemaster
An entertaining film little kids will enjoy, full of positive messages.
on 5+ ★★★★

The Sword in the Stone
Delightful classic brings Arthur legend to life.
on 5+ ★★★★

Elementary School Years (6-10)

The Absent-Minded Professor
Family entertainment at its best.
on 6+ ★★★★★

Aladdin
A magic carpet ride of a movie from Disney.
on 6+ ★★★★★

Annie
Tale of cute orphan is great for the whole family.
on 6+ ★★★★★

Chicken Run
Fabulous animation from Wallace and Gromit creator.
on 6+ ★★★★

Chitty Chitty Bang Bang
A car story custom made for kids.
on 6+ ★★★★

The Indian in the Cupboard
Classic, heartwarming fantasy will rivet kids.
on 6+ ★★★★★

The Little Mermaid
A superbly entertaining animated musical.
on 6+ ★★★★★

March of the Penguins
The penguin movie. A stunning, loving documentary.
on 6+ ★★★★★

Mary Poppins
World's coolest nanny celebrates family and fun.
on 6+ ★★★★★

Miracle on 34th Street
Classic holiday movie for the whole family.
on 6+ ★★★★

Modern Times
Families will cherish Chaplin's silent slapstick.
on 6+ ★★★★★

The Music Man
Glorious production, with gorgeous music, dancing.
on 6+ ★★★★★

My Fair Lady
Tuneful, witty, stylish musical to entertain all ages.
on 6+ ★★★★★

The Nightmare before Christmas
Tim Burton magic with just a touch of scariness.
on 6+ ★★★★★

The Parent Trap
Hayley Mills rocks in her dual role as twins.
on 6+ ★★★★

Pee-wee's Big Adventure
Just as charming and curious as it was in 1985.
on 6+ ★★★★

The Princess Diaries
Terrific fun for girls and their families, too.
on 6+ ★★★★★

Shrek
Gross-out laughs meet a marvelous fairy-tale mix.
on 6+ ★★★★★

Singin' in the Rain
This is often considered the finest musical of all time.
on 6+ ★★★★★

The Sound of Music
Outstanding family film features glorious music.
on 6+ ★★★★★

Wallace and Gromit in Three Amazing Adventures
Witty claymation shorts with whole-family appeal.
on 6+ ★★★★★

The Wizard of Oz
Family classic will send kids over the rainbow.
on 6+ ★★★★★

Angels in the Outfield
Heartwarming movie about hope and baseball.
on 7+ ★★★★

The Dark Crystal
A fantastic but more intense Muppet adventure.
on 7+ ★★★★

E.T. the Extra-Terrestrial
Touching family classic is still one of the best.
on 7+ ★★★★★

Elf
Peppy holiday favorite for both kids and parents.
on 7+ ★★★★

Home Alone
Slapstick family comedy is a new holiday classic.
on 7+ ★★★★

Harry Potter and the Sorcerer's Stone
First Potter movie is a big-budget magical ride.
on 7+ ★★★★★

The Incredibles
Incredible! But action too much for youngest kids.
on 7+ ★★★★★

James and the Giant Peach
Fabulous adaptation of Roald Dahl's classic book.
on 7+ ★★★★

A Little Princess
Wonderful movie of a lonely girl's triumph.
on 7+ ★★★★

Spy Kids
Just the right combination of fantasy and comedy.
on 7+ ★★★★

Yellow Submarine
Beatles classic with great animation and even better music.
on 7+ ★★★★★

Akeelah and the Bee
Inspiring drama about a champion speller.
on 8+ ★★★★

Back to the Future
'80s sci-fi time-travel hit offers laughs and romance.
on 8+ ★★★★★

A Christmas Story
Wonderful antidote to saccharine holiday stories.
on 8+ ★★★★★

Fly Away Home
Thrilling, touching adventure for animal lovers.
on 8+ ★★★★★

Freaky Friday
Mother-daughter switch is fun comedic chaos.
on 8+ ★★★★

A Hard Day's Night
Beatles classic holds up as fabulously as the Fab Four.
on 8+ ★★★★★

Mad Hot Ballroom
Dance documentary hits all the right beats.
on 8+ ★★★★★

The NeverEnding Story
A book-loving boy gets caught up in his own fantasy tale.
on 8+ ★★★★

A Night at the Opera
Marx Brothers masterpiece is still hilarious.
on 8+ ★★★★★

Old Yeller
Tearjerker is one of the best early Disney dramas.
on 8+ ★★★★★

Oliver!
Glorious musical based on *Oliver Twist*.
on 8+ ★★★★☆

The Princess Bride
Witty, winsome fairy tale for the whole family.
on 8+ ★★★★★

Remember the Titans
Inspiring football drama brings history to life.
on 8+ ★★★★☆

Roman Holiday
A delightful classic in romantic Rome.
on 8+ ★★★★★

The Sandlot
Field of Dreams for tweens.
on 8+ ★★★★☆

The Secret of NIMH
Fascinating, but sensitive animal-lovers beware.
on 8+ ★★★★☆

Star Wars: Episode V: The Empire Strikes Back
They're all great. This is the best of the best.
on 8+ ★★★★★

Superman: The Movie
Super-nostalgic adventure still soars.
on 8+ ★★★★☆

Swiss Family Robinson
A good introduction for kids reluctant to watch old movies.
on 8+ ★★★★☆

Willow
Small hero faces huge challenge to save a baby.
on 8+ ★★★★☆

Willy Wonka and the Chocolate Factory
Pure, sweet imagination for both kids and adults.
on 8+ ★★★★★

The Chronicles of Narnia: The Lion, the Witch, and the Wardrobe
Timeless classic faithfully rendered.
on 9+ ★★★★

Hoosiers
A tale of heroic sportsmanship.
on 9+ ★★★★★

Howl's Moving Castle
Charming Miyazaki fairy tale appeals to boys and girls equally.
on 9+ ★★★★

It's a Wonderful Life
This classic delivers warmth all year long.
on 9+ ★★★★★

The Karate Kid
A classic coming-of-age story that remains fresh.
on 9+ ★★★★

Rudy
Inspiring sports film about a real life underdog.
on 9+ ★★★★★

Selena
J-Lo hits the right notes in Tejano star's tale.
on 9+ ★★★★

Walking with Dinosaurs
Dinosaur fans, get ready to snuggle up!
on 9+ ★★★★★

Breaking Away
Rousing bicycle race story is a family favorite.
on 10+ ★★★★

Casablanca
Every kid should see this Bogart classic.
on 10+ ★★★★★

Chariots of Fire
Brilliant true story of 1924 Olympic footrace.
on 10+ ★★★★★

Fiddler on the Roof
Epic portrait of Jewish life during the Russian Revolution.
on 10+ ★★★★★

Ghostbusters
Paranormal fun for the whole family.
on 10+ ★★★★

The Goonies
A classic '80s action-fantasy—tweens will love!
on 10+ ★★★★

Gone with the Wind
We know it, we love it, even fifty-plus years later.
on 10+ ★★★★★

Groundhog Day
A witty, sarcastic take on redemption.
on 10+ ★★★★★

Holes
Great movie respects its audience's intelligence.
on 10+ ★★★★

A League of Their Own
Terrific tweens-and-up story of women's baseball.
on 10+ ★★★★

The Return of the Pink Panther
Hilarious Inspector Clouseau better in this sequel than the original.
on 10+ ★★★★

Pride and Prejudice
Gorgeous Jane Austen adaptation.
on 10+ ★★★★

Spellbound
Every family should see this m-a-r-v-e-l-o-u-s movie.
on 10+ ★★★★★

Spirited Away
Magnificent, spellbinding movie with a bit of an edge.
on 10+ ★★★★★

Young Frankenstein
Brooks' corniness yields plenty of belly laughs.
on 10+ ★★★★★

Tweens, Teens, and Middle Schoolers (11-15)

Drumline Outstanding cast, great message, strong language.	on 11+ ★★★★
Gandhi Brilliant biography that will engage preteens and up.	on 11+ ★★★★★
Little Women Alcott adaptation tugs at your heartstrings.	on 11+ ★★★★
Napoleon Dynamite One-of-a-kind high school comedy for the family.	on 11+ ★★★★
North by Northwest Witty thriller from the master of suspense, Alfred Hitchcock.	on 11+ ★★★★
The Sisterhood of the Traveling Pants Sensitive portrayal of four girls' friendships.	on 11+ ★★★★
Some Like It Hot One of the wildest farces ever.	on 11+ ★★★★★
Spaceballs Goofy parody mocks the *Star Wars* series.	on 11+ ★★★★
Spider-Man A fun movie; may be too intense for younger kids.	on 11+ ★★★★
West Side Story A masterpiece for families to enjoy together.	on 11+ ★★★★★
Whale Rider Excellent to watch and discuss as a family.	on 11+ ★★★★

2001: A Space Odyssey
Kubrick's sci-fi masterpiece is still relevant.

on 12+ ★★★★★

Amadeus
Great movie. Stupidly R for a naked tush and a bit of hanky-panky.

on 12+ ★★★★

Big
Wonderful story with some mature material.

on 12+ ★★★★

Crouching Tiger, Hidden Dragon
Amazing martial arts fairy tale. Magisterial and magical.

on 12+ ★★★★★

The Lord of the Rings: The Fellowship of the Ring
Fabulous, but also violent and scary.

on 12+ ★★★★★

Mrs. Doubtfire
You'll laugh, you'll cry. Best divorce movie.

on 12+ ★★★★

My Big Fat Greek Wedding
The perfect sleepover movie for tween girls (and their moms, too!)

on 12+ ★★★★

Pirates of the Caribbean: The Curse of the Black Pearl
Rip-roaring fun for kids who don't mind skeletons.

on 12+ ★★★★

Raiders of the Lost Ark
A thrill ride and a half.

on 12+ ★★★★★

School of Rock
Standout Jack Black in hilarious nerd-becomes-cool comedy.

on 12+ ★★★★

To Kill a Mockingbird
This masterpiece offers crucial lessons about prejudice.

on 12+ ★★★★★

Title	Description	Age	Rating
American Graffiti	Coming-of-age classic still a must-see for teens.	on 13+	★★★★★
Barbershop	Charming urban comedy for teens.	on 13+	★★★★
Batman Begins	Smart and entertaining, but also very violent.	on 13+	★★★★
Bend It Like Beckham	Superb rendering of a girl's struggle to do what she loves.	on 13+	★★★★
Cinema Paradiso	Charming Italian film about friendship, movies.	on 13+	★★★★
Dead Poets Society	Robin Williams in dramatic role as teacher to troubled boys.	on 13+	★★★★
Edward Scissorhands	Dark yet sweet underdog tale for older kids.	on 13+	★★★★
Grease	Musical phenomenon is great fun but racy.	on 13+	★★★★
Lawrence of Arabia	Mature teens will appreciate this gripping epic.	on 13+	★★★★★
Monty Python and the Holy Grail	Nonstop hilarity for families; some bawdy humor.	on 13+	★★★★★
Of Mice and Men	An elegant adaptation of Steinbeck's classic Depression-era novel.	on 13+	★★★★★
Billy Elliot	Terrific story of a young boy ballet dancer.	on 14+	★★★★

Clueless
Charming, funny take on Jane Austen's *Emma*.
on 14+ ★★★★

The Color Purple
Inspiring, sentimental tale of survival.
on 14+ ★★★★★

Dr. Strangelove, or: How I Learned to Stop Worrying and Love the Bomb
Classic Kubrick black comedy for smart teens and up.
on 14+ ★★★★★

Ferris Bueller's Day Off
Hilarious comedy classic; language makes it PG-13.
on 14+ ★★★★★

Goldfinger
Thrilling action comedy may be the best Bond.
on 14+ ★★★★

Hoop Dreams
Stunning documentary, great family viewing with older kids.
on 14+ ★★★★★

Mean Girls
Mature but often hilarious teen comedy.
on 14+ ★★★★

Real Women Have Curves
Ugly Betty star captivates in teen drama.
on 14+ ★★★★★

This Is Spinal Tap
Hilarious, ribald, drug-filled rock send-up.
on 14+ ★★★★

Moulin Rouge
Dazzling musical romance for teens.
on 15+ ★★★★

Stand by Me
Edgy coming-of-age story not for young kids.
on 15+ ★★★★